EDWARDIAN ENTERPRISE

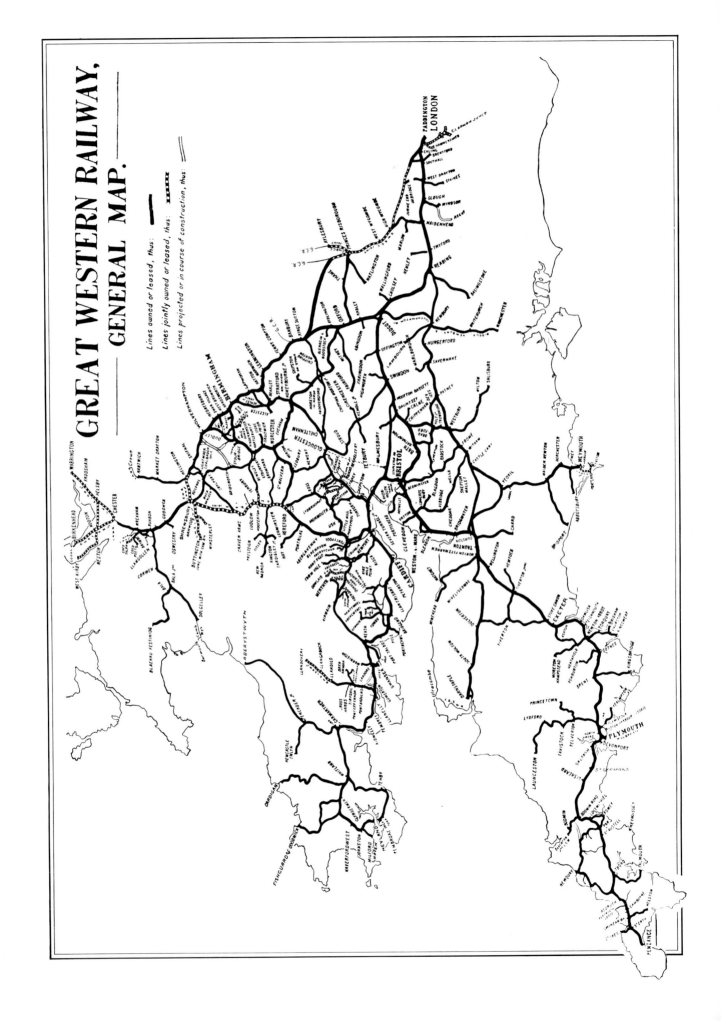

EDWARDIAN ENTERPRISE

A REVIEW OF GREAT WESTERN RAILWAY DEVELOPMENT IN THE FIRST DECADE OF THIS CENTURY

A SERIES OF ESSAYS BY

JOHN NORRIS, GERRY BEALE & JOHN LEWIS

WILD SWAN PUBLICATIONS LTD

FOR
CHRIS TURNER

The authors and publishers would particularly like to thank Chris Turner for all his encouragement and for devoting so much of his time in tracking down a considerable proportion of material used in this book — as usual at the expense of his own research. We would also like to thank Dick Riley, Sean Bolan and Roger Carpenter for so willingly placing their collections at our disposal, and the numerous photographers whose names appear throughout this volume.

Designed by Paul Karau
Typesetting by Berkshire Publishing Services
Printed and bound by Butler & Tanner, Frome

Published by
WILD SWAN PUBLICATIONS LTD.
1-3 Hagbourne Road, Didcot, Oxon OX11 8DP

CONTENTS

FOREWORD

The Edwardian age has long since departed and our way of life and much of our surroundings have changed irrevocably. Few enough people still alive today can recall the time with anything but the memory of a young child, and the majority of us can only glean the spirit of the age from period artefacts, photographs, writings, and, perhaps most immediate of all, music. It would be difficult for any sensitive soul with any awareness of modern history to hear one of Elgar's compositions and not be instantly whisked back to the period and enjoy the images kindled of the England he knew. For that reason it doesn't seem unreasonable to draw the reader's attention to the fact that the Musician Laureate of the Edwardian age was one of the company's clientele — doubtless enjoying the comfort of many a GWR first-class compartment on his journeyings to London from his successive homes in Malvern and Hereford.

Following the 60 year reign of Queen Victoria, during which the embryonic railway system steadily spread its tentacles to link towns and cities throughout the land, came the 'Golden Years' of the Edwardian Era when Britain was at the height of her imperial wealth and power. With hindsight it was indeed a golden age for those with any degree of wealth, a time of prosperity, elegance, hope and blissful unawareness of the gathering clouds on the horizon.

The railways had brought far-reaching benefits to the country as a whole and, in fierce competition with each other, constantly strove to offer improved speed, service, comfort and safety. The GWR was as keen as any to improve and modernise in every way to meet the needs of the twentieth century in style, and in that first decade, the period under review, the ageing Victorian institution that it had become underwent dramatic improvement. Indeed it was the last great period of expansion, the 'Great Awakening' as Macdermot so aptly put it, and, for that matter, the vital stepping stone to most, if not all, subsequent achievements.

By 1910 it was possible to travel from Paddington to Bristol in two hours, reclining in the plush compartments of one of the GWR's latest corridor coaches, hauled by one of the country's most advanced and prestigious 4–6–0s, perhaps dining *en route*. The staff were proud and loyal servants of the company, anxious to please — their job depended on it. The station staff, train crew, signalmen, permanent way men, and all concerned along the route, were also anxious that everything ran smoothly and to time, lateness of a mere two minutes being faithfully recorded in the General Manager's fortnightly reports together with the reason for any delay or hitch.

Before any significant threat from the roads, the Edwardian railway system was the only real means of travel over any distance. The railways had broadened commerce and social activity alike and by this time even provided the working man and his family with a rare opportunity of escape from their daily routine, albeit perhaps only a local journey on market day, or at best an annual day outing to the coast.

In meeting the challenge of the 20th century, there was no time for sentiment in sweeping away any minor legacy from Brunel — just relentless ambition and drive to stride to the very forefront of railway development and offer the best possible service. The results were extremely impressive and if it were possible to step back into 1910 there could surely be very few of us today who would not regard the comfort, service and punctuality with admiration and wonder.

It is not difficult to imagine Sir Edward Elgar smoking one of his pipes while reclining in the sober opulence of a walnut-panelled first-class compartment of a recently commissioned 'toplight' carriage, replete with dark green upholstery, padded arm rests, floral carpet, cord strung luggage racks, and framed views of tempting and idealised locations. Would it really be folly to speculate that while he was enjoying such comfort and idly gazing onto the unspoilt countryside speeding by the windows that, perhaps, just perhaps, one of the themes used in a subsequent composition might have come to him — while travelling on the GWR?

The Great Western Board Room at Paddington. The large map is probably c.1900 as the South Wales and the West of England direct lines are indicated by dots only. *British Railways*

INTRODUCTION

JOHN NORRIS

If comparison is made between a map of the Great Western Railway of 1900 and an equivalent map of the 1980s, one is immediately struck by the extent to which the system had been reduced by the closures of the 1950s and 1960s. But examination will also reveal the existence in 1987 of several main lines which did not exist at the turn of the century. Most were brought into use during the period of Great Western expansion between 1900 and 1910, a decade of development by that company which was to see no equal on the railways of this country until the electrification of the west coast route from London to Scotland during the 1960s.

The new lines which were opened during this period of expansion included the direct line to South Wales through Badminton, the direct line to the West Country through Westbury, and the direct line to the Midlands through Bicester. A new route between Birmingham and Bristol was also brought into use, although this did not survive the rationalisation of recent years, and the section of this route between Honeybourne and Cheltenham will not appear, either on the map of 1900 or that of the 1980s. To all this has to be added the building of a completely new port at Fishguard with its connecting railways, and a diversity of short connecting lines and deviations over the length and breadth of the system.

The whole entailed the construction of more than 250 miles of new line, including 31 miles of joint projects with the Great Central Railway, while another 90 miles of secondary line were upgraded to the standards of a modern main line; much of the latter work entailed conversion from single to double track. Shortly after the end of the decade, but rightly belonging to it, there came the completion of most of the Swansea District Lines which, in particular, gave a direct main line between Neath and Llanelly, avoiding Swansea itself, and so facilitating the working of traffic to and from Fishguard, the coalfields around Llanelly, and the rising holiday resorts on the Pembrokeshire coast.

When Brunel planned his great railway, he certainly made the best possible use of the easy terrain available to him for some ninety miles out of London, but then he reached the long Cotswold escarpment, over which he left a legacy of heavy gradients. There is the long climb at Box on the main line to Bristol, another at Sapperton on his Cheltenham & Great Western Union line, and yet another between Honeybourne and Chipping Campden on the route which he set out for the Oxford, Worcester & Wolverhampton Railway. Elsewhere, heavy gradients are met with in Devon and Cornwall, on the Weymouth line, and between Abergavenny and Llanvihangel on the line from South Wales to Hereford, up which so much coal was worked on its way to the industrial midlands. These gradients added to the journey time of trains, and, with banking engines often available for 24 hours a day as well, they added substantially to operating costs.

Looked at now, the demand for Welsh coal seems to have been almost insatiable. It is true that some of the output in South Wales was hauled away by the LNWR, over both its line from Merthyr and its Central Wales Railway, while a lesser quantity was carried north by the MR via Brecon and Hereford. But the lion's share of the South Wales coal destined for other parts of the kingdom was handled by the GWR. In 1894 the company moved 22,700,000 tons of coal, coke and other minerals; in 1900 the figure was 30,100,000, an increase of one third. To move this prodigious traffic, the company then had no motive power larger than 0—6—0 tender and tank engines; and as there are likely to have been few wagons in use capable of carrying more than ten tons, a large number of relatively light trains had to be worked, increasing track occupation and the time taken in marshalling, and again adding to operating costs.

There had also been a huge growth in passenger traffic. In 1882 47,800,000 passengers used the company's trains, and this figure rose to 65,700,000 in 1894, an increase of over 37%. In 1900 there were 80,900,000 passengers, a further increase of more than 23%.

These traffic volumes were achieved, notwithstanding the reputation which the company had for being the 'Great Way Round'. Between London and the West Country, all traffic had to be routed via Bristol, the only possible alternative being to use the Wilts, Somerset & Weymouth line to Yeovil, thence the single line to Durston, and so to Taunton, a detour to be adopted only in special circumstances. From London to the Midlands and beyond, the route was via Oxford, or the 'Royal Oxford Route' as it was often described in public timetables.

The opening of the Severn Tunnel in 1886 had shortened the distance between London and South Wales, although it necessitated sending traffic via the Bristol area to gain a saving of 15 miles against the traditional route through Gloucester. In practice little could be done to exploit the saving because of the serious congestion around Bristol, and at the turn of the century virtually the whole of the traffic between London and South Wales was still being worked via Gloucester, only the three principal passenger trains each way regularly using the Severn Tunnel. Indeed, at this time it may be questionable whether an adequate return was being obtained on the vast investment of money, manpower and materials, which went to build the tunnel.

A major reason for the congestion in the Bristol area was the amount of traffic using the line between Bristol and Bath over which more than 70 trains were scheduled in each direction every weekday, around 30 of them running to and from Westbury and beyond. Working three trains an hour may seem modest today but there were more stations to serve and local goods trains to accommodate in the timetable. A stopping passenger train from Bristol to Bath was allowed 30 minutes or so for the run of a little more than 11 miles, a long distance goods train rather more. Much of this goods traffic consisted of coal from South Wales for ships at Southampton and Ports-

Coal being worked towards Newport on the Western Valleys section behind a 2—6—2T.   *British Railways*

mouth, often worked by 0—6—0 saddle tank engines the whole way from Aberdare to Salisbury, where it was handed over to the LSWR.

A timetable will never reveal the true volume of traffic handled as special trains were frequently required, many at short notice. In December 1904 the *Times* reported that during international tension in the previous month, the GWR had worked to Portland nearly 3,000 tons of coal in three days for bunkering the Channel fleet. Other special traffic may have been more predictable in its timing but, nonetheless, placed a strain on the resources of the company, not least of all in track occupation, which was often aggravated by the need to move trains of empty rolling stock to the places where it was needed. Seasonal crops of fruit, vegetables and flowers had to be handled, whether they be the produce of local growers in Cornwall and the Vale of Evesham, or the produce of growers in the Channel Islands and the Scillies arriving at Weymouth and Penzance. The level of such seasonal traffic may be judged from a report that no less than 38 special trains for spring vegetables were run from stations in Cornwall during a

single week in April 1907. Also requiring special facilities were the big ships which were making their appearance on the transatlantic services and which called at Plymouth eastbound to disembark passengers and mails.

The volume of traffic, the limited locomotive power, and the gradients on some of the busiest sections of the line were all challenges to be faced as the 20th century drew near. But they were not the only challenges, because the user of the railway himself was becoming more demanding as to the facilities provided. In the summer of 1899 the corridor passenger train was still very much the exception on all but the most important services, while restaurant cars were provided on only three such trains each way in and out of Paddington, and none elsewhere on the system. Steam heating in winter was in use on the corridor trains but its general application had yet to come, although it had freshly become a standard installation on all new coaching stock. If the GWR did not offer improvements, other companies would rapidly do so, the LSWR on its services to the west, the LNWR to the midland cities. Competition was very real, and the LSWR already had the edge over the GWR in timings between London and Exeter, while the LNWR could readily take advantage of its shorter distance between London and Birmingham.

Many large towns were still poorly served. Suffice it to quote the case of Swansea, situated at the end of what had become a short branch from Landore, where so many of its passengers had to change, whether they be travelling into West Wales, or east towards Cardiff and London. In

seem that the majority had been keen to take up the additional shares offered to them.

But above all, the company had men able to face the challenges before them. During the years when so many of the vital decisions had to be taken at board level, the directors had in their chairman, Earl Cawdor, a man of the highest calibre, and it was from him that so much of the inspiration came for transforming the Great Western

4–4–0 locomotive No. 3408, freshly renamed *Killarney*, poses with 70 ft concertina coaches for the Fishguard boat train. The boards on the leading coach read 'Irish Express via Fishguard'.
British Railways

the summer of 1899 there were only two trains which would see a passenger into Swansea from Paddington, 201 miles, in under five hours, and one of these was the boat train to New Milford which ran on three days a week only.

Planning for the great expansion had started long before 1900, and several of the private bills needed to give the company power to undertake the works had passed through parliament and received the royal assent during the 1890s. The task of raising the necessary finance may be said to have begun in 1896, continuing gradually until 1908 as the various schemes progressed. During those 13 years, shares and stock to a nominal value of £14,100,000 were issued, but such was the strength of the company that these issues attracted an average premium of over 40%, which brought in a further sum of £5,900,000. The relative ease with which the company could raise capital meant that it did not have to resort to the issue of preference shares as a desperate means of attracting investors, while borrowings on debenture rose by only £3,000,000 during the same period, well within the statutory limits. In 1907 it was reported that the company had over 30,000 stockholders, and it would

system. Closely associated with the chairman was James C. Inglis, through whose hands as chief engineer since 1892, so much of the planning had passed, and when a new general manager came to be appointed in 1903 to succeed the late Sir Joseph Wilkinson, it was to Inglis that the board turned; in his new capacity, he served the company with distinction, implementing the many opportunities offered by the new works to the greatest possible effect. George Jackson Churchward was shortly to become the company's chief mechanical engineer, a man whose thinking was to have a profound influence on locomotive design for many years to come. However, this almost legendary figure, discussed later in Chapter 5, has tended to overshadow Inglis's achievements by reason of the interest in the steam locomotive rather than in the railway as a whole, denying full justice to the man who played such a large part in the expansion of the Great Western Railway during the Edwardian era.

The name of Isambard Kingdom Brunel is known to millions of people, few of whom have even a passing interest in railways, and it is to Brunel that credit is justifiably given for the creation of much of the GWR system. But as this study tries to show, a large part of that

Frederick, Third Earl Cawdor (formerly Viscount Emlyn) — a director of the Great Western Railway Company from 1890 to 1905, and its chairman from 1895 to 1905.   *British Railways*

system was built long after Brunel's death and was not even conceived by him. The man who probably did most for the company in its great leap forward was James Charles Inglis.

Inglis was a Scot, born at Aberdeen in 1851, and educated at the grammar school and university there. After practical experience in the engineering shops of a company in Glasgow, he became a pupil to the consulting engineer to the Alexandra (Newport) Dock Company, and following completion of the first dock in 1875, he took up employment with the South Devon Railway at Plymouth, where he was engaged on construction of deep-water quays and other works at the Millbay Docks. He was also involved with doubling of sections of single line on both the South Devon and Cornwall Railways. The days of the South Devon Railway as a separate entity were drawing to a close, however, and shortly after the completion of its amalgamation with the GWR in 1878 he resigned his appointment to take up practice as a consulting engineer in Plymouth.

His practice brought him more dock work at Plymouth, as well as work in the enlargement of Newlyn Harbour in Cornwall. He was not at a loss in dealing with railway construction, being responsible for the works of the Princetown Railway Company, while he also undertook work for the GWR, including the construction of its branch to Bodmin and the rebuilding of some of the Brunel timber viaducts. In June 1892 he took up employment with the GWR once more, four months later he was appointed its chief engineer, and in 1903 he was appointed general manager and consulting engineer.

In his position of chief engineer, Inglis did not have much time to settle in and take stock of the tasks before him. Revised plans for the works on the Berks & Hants

Extension from Hungerford to Patney & Chirton, and for the new line from there to Westbury, had to be ready for the parliamentary session of 1893-4. For the session of 1895-6 plans went forward for the first of the major challenges, the South Wales & Bristol Direct Line.

The promoters of the direct line of 1865 had employed Sir John Fowler as their consulting engineer, and the GWR now employed him in a similar capacity for the revised scheme. However, when the new plans were deposited, they bore the name of Inglis alongside that of Fowler. It cannot be denied that the completed work was a triumph for Inglis, but sadly his name will be scarcely known to those who travel over it in modern high-speed trains at two miles a minute, a speed of which Inglis can hardly have dreamed.

When it came to the plans for the line from Cheltenham to Honeybourne in 1898, they bore the name of Inglis alone, and it is likely that other sets of plans were similar. On the same man would fall the responsibility of cross-examination on the plans before parliamentary committees.

So much of what will be described in these pages will have passed through the hands of Inglis before it reached the directors for approval that it is hard to conceive that he had the time and the energy for outside interests, but he had several involvements. He was a governor of the London School of Economics, and a member of the Royal Commission on Canals & Inland Waterways. In 1908 he was elected President of the Institution of Civil Engineers, and he accepted office for a second term in the following year — an unusual honour. He was knighted in the New Year Honours for 1911. By then his health was giving cause for concern, and he passed away at Rottingdean, near Brighton, on 19th December of the same year. He was buried at the Kensington Cemetry at Hanwell.

An obituary in the Institution of Civil Engineers Minutes of Proceedings records: 'In personal character Sir James was eminently practical, with a mechanic's instinct to recognize that which rang true. He was thorough, broad in his views, alike in engineering and in his more private opinions. A Liberal-Unionist in politics, he was an Imperialist in the highest sense of the word. Kindly and warm-hearted, he did much to encourage others both in business and in private life.'

What might have been his greatest triumph — the establishment of Fishguard as a port with full facilities for ocean liners — never came to fruition, and he did not live to hear of the abandonment of the later works which had been planned under his direction. There had also been plans for extensive new harbour works at Weymouth, which had passed through parliament in 1898; these, too, were abandoned by the directors in 1912. His confidence in shipping services to Brest and Nantes seems also to have been misplaced. On matters such as these, his optimism clearly died with him, not shared by those who remained to manage the great company for which he had accomplished so much else.

Perhaps one day the biography of James Inglis will be written, giving full justice to the man who played such a large part in the expansion of the Great Western Railway during the Edwardian era.

SIR JAMES INGLIS

Badminton station, looking west.

British Railways

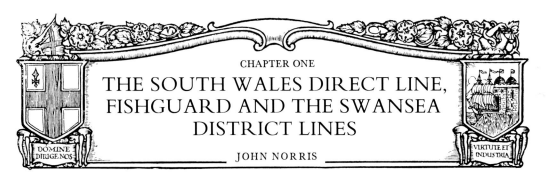

CHAPTER ONE

THE SOUTH WALES DIRECT LINE,
FISHGUARD AND THE SWANSEA
DISTRICT LINES

JOHN NORRIS

OF the several new lines, probably the one most urgently needed was the South Wales Direct Line. The idea for such a line was certainly not new because a company had been incorporated in 1865 with power to build a South Wales & Great Western Direct Railway, connecting the South Wales line of the GWR near Chepstow with its main line at Wootton Bassett, a distance of 41 miles. The scheme entailed bridging the Severn in the vicinity of the site of the modern road bridge between Beachley and Aust. The directors included powerful South Wales interests, among them Christopher Rice Mansel Talbot, a former chairman of the South Wales Railway, and the driving force behind the building of the docks near Aberavon which were named after him as Port Talbot. The economic climate of the time was not right for raising the large amount of capital needed, however, and the scheme was abandoned.

In 1895 South Wales interests, with the Barry Railway Company to the fore, petitioned parliament for leave to bring in a bill for a London & South Wales Railway, a much more elaborate scheme than that of 1865. Leaving the Barry Railway at Cogan, its planned route embodied several connections in the Cardiff area with both the Taff Vale Railway and the railways of the Bute Docks, then in the neighbourhood of Newport with both the Brecon & Merthyr Railway and the GWR. After crossing the Severn between Beachley and Aust, the line was projected to cross the MR at Wickwar, making connections in all four directions, and then to make two connections with the MSWJR which it was to cross north of Cricklade. No more connections with other railways were proposed before the line diverged near Bledlow, one branch continuing to join the future GCR at Great Missenden, and the other to pass through High Wycombe and Ruislip on its way to meet the MR south of Hendon. The engineers for the scheme included Sir James W. Szlumper and his brother, Alfred W. Szlumper; both had been involved already with railway building in South Wales, but Alfred was to become chief engineer of the LSWR, while his son, Gilbert, became general manager of the Southern Railway in 1937.

The GWR was hardly caught unawares by this intrusion. Its plans for a line from Wootton Bassett to give direct access to the approaches to the Severn Tunnel at Patchway, with a curve from Stoke Gifford to join the existing line from the tunnel to Bristol, were sufficiently far advanced for a bill to be presented to parliament for the session of 1896, when the proposals of the London & South Wales promoters were also to be considered. In due course the latter withdrew, and the GWR obtained powers for the construction of 30 miles of new line, described as

the 'South Wales & Bristol Direct Railway'. No time was lost in implementing the powers, and the first sod was cut with due ceremony by the Dowager Duchess of Beaufort at Old Sodbury in November 1897.

The work of construction was to take more than five years but the outcome was to be a length of railway, brilliantly conceived and the model for the other new lines which were to follow. The summit of the Cotswold escarpment was crossed by a mile of level track with the station for Badminton at its western end, and this was approached in either direction by a rise of ten miles or so on a gradient of 1 in 300. Indeed, with only one negligible exception, there was no gradient steeper than this on the whole line, a remarkable achievement compared with the climb of 1 in 100 eastward through Box on the original line. A major factor in securing the easier gradients was Sodbury tunnel, 4,444 yards in length to the West of Badminton, together with Alderton tunnel of 506 yards on the eastern side. Both tunnels were built in a perfectly straight line, thus helping ventilation, while other careful planning had allowed a short length of level track to be left near Chipping Sodbury for the installation of water troughs.

To the modest gradients there has to be added another notable feature in that the line was built with no curve having a radius of less than one mile. The concept of a line for fast long-distance running was completed by building four of the seven intermediate stations with four running lines through them; thus a slower train could stand on one of the outer lines serving the platforms while faster trains overtook on the centre lines, itself an economy of operation, hitherto little practised, compared with the traditional time-consuming reversal of trains into refuge sidings. The stations with four running lines were those at Little Somerford, Badminton, Chipping Sodbury and Coalpit Heath.

The new line was opened for local goods traffic from Wootton Bassett as far as Badminton on 1st January 1903, and on 1st May in the same year it was opened throughout for goods traffic, including the heavy long-distance trains for which it had been intended. To assist in the marshalling of trains, extensive new yards were laid out at Stoke Gifford. These provided much-needed relief for the existing yards in Bristol, but they also enabled mineral traffic arriving from South Wales through the Severn Tunnel to be made up into much heavier trains for conveyance eastwards.

Passenger traffic began on 1st July 1903 and there was an immediate improvement in the times from Paddington to the cities and towns of South Wales. Cardiff was reached

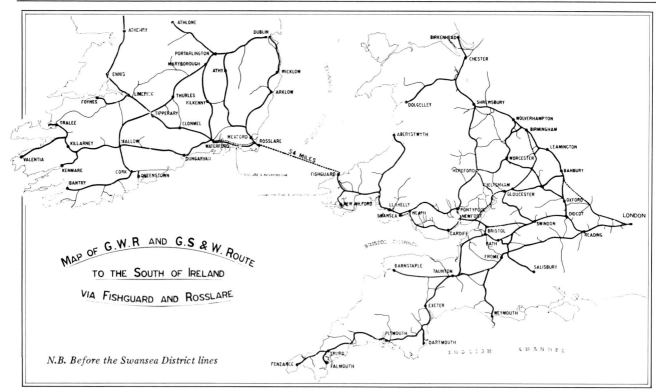

MAP OF G.W.R AND G.S & W. ROUTE
TO THE SOUTH OF IRELAND
VIA FISHGUARD AND ROSSLARE

N.B. Before the Swansea District lines

in 2 hrs 55 mins by three trains daily, while in one instance the time to Swansea came down to 4 hrs 15 mins. By the summer of 1910 further savings of up to twelve minutes had been made. The railway company was then looking at a new market, the business traveller, and the schedules enabled a business man to travel from South Wales to London and back very comfortably in the day, having breakfast on the train on his outward journey, and dinner on his return. While the saving in distance between Paddington and South Wales was ten miles, compared with the route via Bath, it was the very nature of the new route which contributed most to the improved timings. For Bristol, too, the new line had advantages, and trains to Paddington not required to stop at Bath had the benefit of an easier route, as was often demonstrated in later years by the running of the up 'Bristolian'.

One other advantage afforded to the new line was the relatively small potential for local traffic, as a result of which it could be kept largely clear of stopping trains. Only Badminton was likely to generate much traffic, and it was served by a small number of the long-distance trains as well as by the local trains, normally running between Swindon and Bristol. Had there been more population, it is likely that the area would have been served by railways long before, in which case the concept of the South Wales & Bristol Direct Railway would have been quite different.

Much as the new railway was needed for the traffic of South Wales and Bristol, the GWR had other plans with which it would be of use, and these involved the development of Fishguard as a port. Fishguard Bay was a fine natural harbour on the north side of the Pembrokeshire peninsula, but it was little used. Small craft went to a

quay in the south-east corner of the bay at the old town of Fishguard, while little more than a few local fishing boats operated from the village of Goodwick in the south-west corner. The South Wales Railway had planned to build a new port for Ireland in Fishguard Bay, but this was abandoned in favour of a site on the opposite side of the peninsula at the village of Neyland, or New Milford as it came to be known.

The watershed running roughly from east to west across the peninsula is much closer to the north side than to the south, and so it was easier for the South Wales Railway to make its approach into the district on the south side, even though it meant that a difficult route would have to be engineered over the high ground if Fishguard were to be adopted as the port. This factor, coupled with the cost and length of time in building a completely new port there, led the South Wales directors to choose Neyland instead, although not before a small amount of work had been done on building the railway towards Fishguard.

We may pick up the story of the development of Fishguard in 1895 when two companies were involved, both under the control of two Victorian entrepreneurs from Birmingham, where each company had its registered office. The companies were the North Pembrokeshire & Fishguard Railway, and the Fishguard & Rosslare Railways & Harbours.

The Rosslare company already owned railways in Ireland, together with a partly-constructed harbour at Rosslare. It also had powers, as yet unexercised, to build a pier, breakwater and embankment in Fishguard Bay. It was about to acquire a steamboat from the Belfast Steam-

Construction work in progress on the breakwater at Fishguard.
GWR Magazine

ship Company; this was the S.S. *Voltaic* of 580 gross registered tons, and, although nearly thirty years old, the company proceeded to operate a service with it between Rosslare, Liverpool and Bristol.

The North Pembrokeshire company owned a steeply-graded and circuitous single line of railway from Clynderwen to Letterston, a distance of 17¼ miles, and it had powers to complete this railway from Letterston through to Goodwick. A railway was, of course, essential to the success of the marine works at Fishguard but with gradients as steep as 1 in 27, an easier route would have to be found, and deviations were authorised in 1895 and 1897. It was also necessary to obtain the support and co-operation of one of the major companies. Having failed to gain the backing of the GWR, the North Pembrokeshire proceeded to obtain powers to build its Narberth & Carmarthen Extension, which would link its existing line with the LNWR branch from Llandilo to Carmarthen at Abergwli.

The threat of intervention by the LNWR provided the spur for what the gentlemen from Birmingham had hoped — a take-over by the GWR. In the event, an Act of 1898 allowed the Rosslare company to become jointly owned by the GWR and the Great Southern & Western Railway of Ireland, but being in a majority of 4 to 3 at the board table, the GWR was left in a controlling situation. Soon after the change in control, the registered office of the company was transferred to Paddington, and the *Voltaic* was sold to other parties in Liverpool.

The immediate purpose of the two owning companies was to establish a new short sea route as soon as possible — 54 miles from Fishguard to Rosslare, compared with 98 miles on the service operated by the GWR from New Milford to Waterford. To this end the agreement between the companies provided for each to undertake responsibility for executing the works required on its own side of the St. George's Channel. Financial responsibility was divided equally between them.

The difficulties facing the GWR engineers were enormous. The new quays were to be built on the west side of

A charge of explosive brings down rock from the cliff face at Fishguard as a way is made for the quays and railway installations.
GWR Magazine

Fishguard Bay, commencing at the end of the village of Goodwick, along a line of the cliffs which rose almost sheer from the water to a height of as much as 200 feet. The facilities for bringing in by sea the machinery and equipment for the works were minimal, while by rail the nearest point of delivery was still Letterston, whence there was a hard haul over inadequate roads. The need to complete the North Pembrokeshire Railway from Letterston to Goodwick was urgent, therefore, and the section was opened on 1st July 1899.

The first task of the engineers was to blast rock from the cliffs to leave what, in effect, was a ledge a little above water level on which to build the quays, a new station,

Laying the first block of the quay wall at Fishguard, 10th October 1903.   *GWR Magazine*

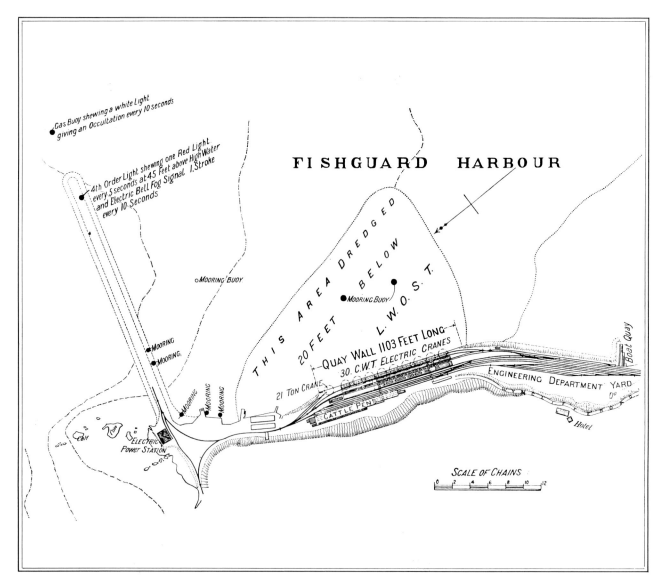

Gas Buoy shewing a white Light giving an Occultation every 10 seconds

4th Order Light shewing one Red Light every 5 seconds at 45 Feet above High Water and Electric Bell Fog Signal 1.Stroke every 10 Seconds

FISHGUARD   HARBOUR

Mooring Buoy

THIS AREA DREDGED 20 FEET BELOW L.W.O.S.T.

Mooring Buoy

MOORING
MOORING
MOORING
MOORING
MOORING

Quay Wall 1103 Feet Long
30 C.W.T. ELECTRIC CRANES
21 Ton Crane

CATTLE PENS

ENGINEERING DEPARTMENT YARD

Boat Quay

Hotel

Coir
ELECTRIC POWER STATION

SCALE OF CHAINS
0   2   4   6   8   10   12

Looking out along the breakwater with the harbour works at an advanced stage. Empty ballast wagons occupy much of the foreground, and beyond them other wagons stand at a sawmill. In the bottom right-hand corner part of the stone crusher may be seen.

British Railways

Much of the site for the quay has been cleared, and rails wait to be laid.

British Railways

The Fishguard Bay Hotel, previously the Wyncliff Hotel, which was in existence before the construction of the harbour, and which had been acquired by the Fishguard & Rosslare company at an early stage in its history.

British Railways

sidings, warehouses, and approach roads and railways. There was little or no foothold on the cliff face and it was generally necessary to lower men on ropes from the cliff top to bore holes in the rock by hand, in which to place small charges of explosive. Work went on in this way for about six years during which time nearly 500,000 tons of rock had been removed. Of that total, most (about 400,000 tons) was used as filling along the water's edge for the quay, while the remainder was largely used to commence construction of the breakwater.

Although the progress so far had been very slow, there had been made available a narrow strip of land on which engines, cranes and wagons could be employed, but the work had to be speeded if the intentions of opening the new port were to be realised in anything like a reasonable time. Accordingly, additional plant was brought to the site, and improved blasting techniques were adopted, one mammoth charge being reported to have brought down 113,000 tons of rock alone. The ultimate total of rock removed was about 2,500,000 tons. Construction of a breakwater, extending 2,000 feet into the bay to protect

the quays, took about 1,250,000 tons of material, mainly rock from the cliff face in pieces ranging from 5 tons to 27 tons on the seaward side, and up to 3 tons each on the landward.

Quite clearly the former North Pembrokeshire Railway was totally inadequate to provide rail access to Fishguard when the port became operational, even if the authorised deviations were made and other improvements carried out. Accordingly, a completely new line was planned, following very much the course of that originally intended by Brunel for the South Wales Railway more than fifty years before. Indeed, for a short distance from the junction with the existing line to New Milford at Clarbeston Road, it is said that the new line used earthworks and a bridge which had been constructed for the South Wales Railway before the decision was taken to abandon Fishguard in favour of New Milford.

At Letterston Junction the new line met the North Pembrokeshire which it was to use for the remainder of its distance to Goodwick, about four miles. This section was doubled from the junction as far as Manorwen, but

Fishguard Harbour station shortly before the commencement of services.   *Cty. Railway Gazette*

Goodwick soon after the opening of the harbour. The new locomotive shed may be seen centre, while the station, known as 'Fishguard & Goodwick', may be seen bottom left.

Collection Paul Karau

from there to Goodwick it was allowed to remain single in view of an expectation that a completely new line on easier gradients would ultimately be built for the use of up trains only. This expectation was never realised so that heavy boat trains leaving Fishguard Harbour are still immediately confronted with a climb, including two miles mainly at 1 in 50, to cross the watershed so near to the north side of the peninsula.

Over and above the port works and the railway on the Welsh side, the GWR took responsibility for the purchase of three new ships for the Irish service. It had, of course, an established marine department, and in 1902 it had taken delivery of two new ships for the service to Waterford from New Milford; these were the *Great Western* and the *Great Southern*. For the Fishguard-Rosslare service the three ships ordered were the *St. David*, the *St. George*, and the *St. Patrick*. The *St. George* was built at Birkenhead by Cammell, Laird & Co. Ltd., the other two on the Clyde by John Brown & Co. Ltd. A fourth ship, the *St. Andrew*, was ordered in June 1907 from the yard of John Brown, and this was completed in April 1908. All were built of steel, and had triple screw driven by steam turbines, with eight boilers working at 185 lbs per sq. in. They varied slightly in detail, as is shown by the following particulars taken from Lloyd's Register:-

	St. Andrew	St. David	St. George	St. Patrick
Gross tonnage	2528	2529	2456	2531
Length	351.1 ft	350.8 ft	352.0 ft	350.8 ft
Breadth	41.1 ft	41.1 ft	41.1 ft	41.1 ft
Depth	16.5 ft	16.5 ft	16.2 ft	16.5 ft

Accommodation was provided on board for a total of 1000 passengers, including 220 first-class sleeping berths, and 100 second-class. Master of the *St. Andrew* in 1912 was Capt. J. S. Burnand whose name appears as master of the *Voltaic* during the time of its ownership by the Rosslare Company.

The reason for ordering the *St. Andrew* is unclear as it would seem adequate to have had one vessel spare against the two in service, each making six round voyages a week as was required. It is, of course, possible that the *St. George*, which was stated to be the first turbine vessel to be built by Cammell, Laird & Co. Ltd. at Birkenhead, was not entirely satisfactory. In 1912, however, the number of vessels for the service reverted to three upon the sale of the *St. George* to the Canadian Pacific Railway; it returned to United Kingdom registry in 1919 upon acquisition by the GER, seeing service between Harwich and the Hook of Holland and Antwerp.

By the summer of 1906 it was possible to plan the opening of the new service and on Thursday, 23rd August, guests were taken from London to be entertained on board the *St. David* overnight at Fishguard. Other guests arrived next morning on board the *St. Patrick* on its maiden voyage from Glasgow, and this ship was used to convey the entire party to Rosslare and back later that day. The public service commenced on 30th August, and the services from New Milford to both Waterford and Cork were transferred to Fishguard on the same day.

The GWR certainly made great efforts to ensure the success of the new service, which provided a day and a night crossing in each direction, daily except Sundays.

Boat trains left Paddington at 8.45 a.m. and 8.45 p.m., each taking 5½ hours to Fishguard, where they arrived in time to work the equivalent return service. The speed of handling passengers, baggage and mails was a matter of great pride to the company, no more than 15 minutes being allowed between the arrival time of the train and the sailing time of the ship, and vice versa.

New coaching stock was built for the trains which carried nameboards in gold lettering on a red ground, 'Irish Express via Fishguard' (for the day service), and 'Irish Mail via Fishguard' (for the night service). Full catering facilities were available on both trains, and a sleeping car was included in the formation of the night train. A female attendant travelled on the trains to give any assistance needed by lady passengers and children. Passengers on the night service who did not wish to be disturbed when the ship arrived at Fishguard in the small hours, could remain on board until 8.00 a.m. Very much for their benefit, a train was run from the harbour station to Clarbeston Road, where a connecting service was available to all the principal stations to Cardiff and Paddington.

Widespread publicity was given to all these facilities, and to the connections available at Cardiff with other parts of the system. One notable example of the connecting services was a restaurant car express between Cardiff and Birmingham, running via Hereford and Worcester. This left Cardiff soon after the arrival of the morning service from Fishguard, with the return working at 7.05 p.m. from Birmingham to connect into the boat train from Paddington. In the down direction this train was described in Bradshaw as 'South Wales & Irish Mail Express'.

With four vessels at the company's disposal, thoughts quickly turned to the introduction of excursion sailings and other seasonal services. Douglas (Isle of Man) was a popular destination for long day excursions, in connection with which special trains were run from the principal stations in South Wales. These excursions carried near-capacity loadings of around 1,000 passengers, and many people were often unable to obtain tickets. For the summer season of 1911 a service was operated each Saturday to Douglas. Another port where the Fishguard ships were seen from time to time was Dublin. Shorter excur-

St. David, the first of the new steamers to be seen at Fishguard.

Cty. Railway Gazette

One of the new turbine steamers at her berth, while three other steamers lie at the quays. In the centre a rake of four- or six-wheeled vehicles stand at the outer face of the platform, probably a train for Clynderwen via the Rosebush line.

BBC Hulton Picture Library

In this peaceful scene across Fishguard Bay, railway interest centres on the cattle trucks, waiting to receive livestock arriving from Ireland.

GWR Magazine

The cattle pens adjoining the quays.

British Railways

Fishguard Harbour station on the opening day, 30th August 1906.

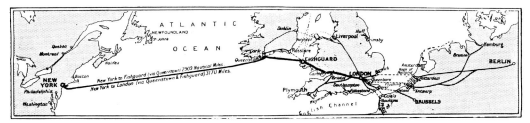

Sketch Map of the New Short Route, New York to London and the Continent.

sions were operated round the coast to places such as Neyland and Tenby, but for these the smaller vessels used as tenders could be employed.

As part of its summer programme for 1907, the GWR instituted a series of excursions from Paddington to the lakes of Southern Ireland. These involved travel by special train to Fishguard on a Friday evening to connect with the night crossing to Rosslare, returning in the same way on the Saturday night. The trains were booked from Paddington to Fishguard without an intermediate stop in five hours, a run made possible by the installation of water troughs near Magor and near Ferryside, as well as from improvements to the track west of Cardiff. They received considerable publicity, enhanced by the naming of a 4—4—0 locomotive *Killarney*, intended to work them.

The publicity for these trains was directed much more widely than to the potential excursionist, however, as the GWR was keen to demonstrate to shipping companies its ability to run non-stop trains of this nature as one means of attracting ocean liners to Fishguard, something which the company had had very much in mind throughout its involvement with the port. Although there was a depth of 30 feet of water in the bay in places little more than 400 yards from the shore, it would not be possible to bring such vessels to the quays, but the transfer of passengers, baggage and mails could be undertaken by tender as at Plymouth, at least for the time being.

The first practical test of the ability of the company to handle an ocean liner came on 2nd April 1908 when the S.S. *Lanfranc* of the Booth line called at Fishguard, homeward bound to Liverpool from South America. The company came through the test with distinction. A special train, albeit only three coaches and a van hauled by the 4—4—0 locomotive *Maine*, left Fishguard barely fifty minutes after the liner had dropped anchor in the bay. The non-stop journey to Paddington took 4 hrs 56 mins. Similar arrangements were made for the S.S. *Antony* of the Booth line on 23rd April, and that company's ships continued to call at around monthly intervals.

But there were bigger prizes to be won in the form of traffic from Cunard liners on the eastward run from New York to Liverpool. The White Star Line had commenced to disembark passengers at Holyhead, enabling them to reach their destinations rather sooner than if they had completed their voyages to Liverpool. In 1909 the Cunard company decided to respond to the competition set by the White Star in association with the LNWR, and accordingly it was arranged that its ships should call at Fishguard. Considerable play was made on the fact that Fishguard

was nearer (by about 40 miles) to New York than any other port in Great Britain. It was also convenient for ships to call there, particularly if they were calling at Queenstown in Southern Ireland as well.

It is conceivable that the Cunard company had been interested in the possibilities of Fishguard as a port for rather longer than these developments may suggest because Bradshaw Shareholders' Manual for the years 1896-1899 records one, E. H. Cunard, as a director of the North Pembrokeshire & Fishguard Railway. His address is given as Palmerston Buildings, Bishopsgate Street, London E.C., where the Cunard company had its head office at the time. In 1907 he joined the GWR board following the

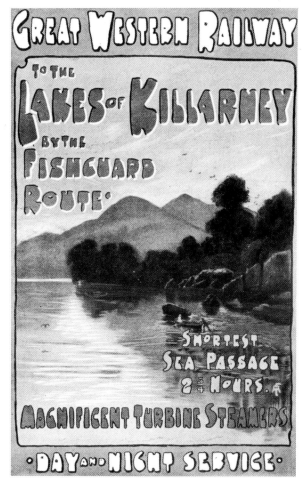

The RMS *Mauretania* arriving in Fishguard Bay on her maiden call on 30th August 1909.

British Railways

Fishguard

THE NEW PORT OF CALL FOR
OCEAN LINERS.

The Shortest Route from
New York to London.

NEW YORK

LONDON

Customs Officials.

G.P.O. Staff.

Railway Staff.

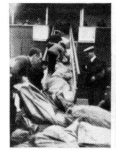

Taking the Mails in the Tender

The "Cunard Ocean Mail."

Passengers Embarking on the Tender—leaving—and arriving at the Quay.

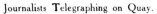

Journalists Telegraphing on Quay.

The Customs Examination.

SNAPSHOTS AT FISHGUARD, AUGUST 30th, 1909.

A first-class coach at Fishguard for the 'Cunard Ocean Express, Fishguard-London', one of the last clerestory coaches to be built by the GWR.   *BBC Hulton Picture Library*

Some of the first passengers to disembark from a Cunard liner at Fishguard wait to board their train to Paddington.

BBC Hulton Picture Library

A special train for the inaugural call of the R.M.S. *Mauretania* at Fishguard leaves for Cardiff and Paddington on 30th August 1909.
BBC Hulton Picture Library

death of a long-serving director, David MacIver, who had had important shipping interests. E. H. Cunard subsequently became one of the GWR nominees on the board of the Fishguard & Rosslare Railways & Harbours Company.

The first call by a Cunard liner was that of the R.M.S. *Mauretania* on Monday, 30th August 1909, three years to the day after the commencement of the Irish service. The big ship arrived in the bay at 1.20 p.m. and was at anchor for no more than 40 minutes, but this was sufficient to enable a special train with the mails to leave at 2.08 p.m. Special passenger trains followed at 2.53 p.m. and 3.05 p.m., reaching Paddington in 4 hrs 35 mins and 4 hrs 51 mins respectively. Each of the passenger trains was worked by a pair of 4—4—0 locomotives from Fishguard to Cardiff, there replaced by a 4—6—0 of the 'Star' class.

In addition to the *Mauretania*, a number of famous names among the Cunard fleet became regular visitors to Fishguard — *Lusitania, Campania, Carmania, Caronia, Carpathia* among others. Times were variable, however, but for the GWR the ideal was a mid-afternoon arrival, from which they could deliver passengers at Paddington at a comfortable hour, whereas those passengers who continued their voyage to Liverpool might not reach London until the following day. On other occasions, when transfer to the tender may have arisen in the small hours of the morning, passengers may well have preferred to go through to Liverpool. It was not unknown for two liners to call within a few hours of each other, and on a day in September 1909 four special trains are reported to have made the run to Paddington, each in about 4¾ hours.

James Inglis and, it is believed, the resident engineer of Fishguard Harbour, Mr. G. Lambert Gibson.
BBC Hulton Picture Library

At the conclusion of a record-breaking round trip by the *Mauretania* in December 1910, 598 passengers and 3177 bags of mail were dealt with at Fishguard, and for the year as a whole it was reported that 14,300 passengers and 55,800 bags of mail were landed from Cunard ships. From time to time, too, there were reports of bullion being landed. In 1911 passengers on the Cunard service from Boston were also given the option of disembarking at Fishguard.

For the Cunard company there was also competition from other European shipping companies on the transatlantic route, as some of their ships called at Plymouth to disembark passengers before continuing to French or German ports. However, Cunard was aware that if a passenger could be conveyed speedily overland to one of the ports on the English Channel, he could continue his journey by the short sea route, and often gain time as compared with the sea voyage from America to, say, Bremen or Cherbourg. Accordingly, with the co-operation

A restaurant car, Cunard Special.   *Topical*

Scene at Paddington in May 1911 upon the arrival of a Cunard Ocean Express with passengers from Boston. *BBC Hulton Picture Library*

of the SE & CR, the GWR would arrange a special train from Fishguard to Dover, if the number of passengers justified it. A few days before the first call by the R.M.S. *Mauretania* the *Times* reported that GWR coaches had been tested for clearance on the Admiralty Pier at Dover, adding that when a special train was required, it would run via the West London line and Herne Hill. It is believed that special nameboards were prepared for such trains shortly before the war of 1914, but never used. Even without a special train to Dover, it was readily possible for a passenger who arrived at Fishguard in a morning to take the boat train to Paddington, travel from Charing Cross to Folkestone in the afternoon, and be in Paris the same evening.

The GWR was under no illusions that to develop fully the potential of Fishguard Bay as an Atlantic port, berthing facilities would have to be provided. The transfer of incoming mails from ship to tender was a relatively simple operation by shute, but transfer from tender to ship was more difficult and time-consuming, and required the use of lifting gear on the ship. Nonetheless, the Blue Funnel liner *Aeneas*, outward bound from Glasgow to Australia, called at Fishguard on Saturday, 19 November 1910, to embark passengers, becoming the first liner to do so. The times permitted a special train to be run from Paddington that morning, whereas passengers from London would have needed to leave on the Thursday evening to join the ship at Glasgow. Other ships of the Blue Funnel line to call at Fishguard outward bound in the following year included the *Anchises* and the *Ascanius*. In 1912, however, the company adopted Liverpool as its main port of embarkation and the call at Fishguard was regarded as unnecessary.

In August 1911 the S.S. *Highland Warrior* of the Nelson line, bound for South America, embarked passengers at Fishguard, and a special train carrying about 150 passengers was run from Paddington. The circumstances appear to have been exceptional, however, as the ship had recently been constructed at Greenock, and the call was probably made to avoid sending it to London, which would have been its normal port of embarkation.

Scarcely had the excitement over the start of the Irish service died down before plans were being laid for additional works at Fishguard. In 1908 powers were obtained for the construction of a second breakwater extending upwards of one mile in a north-easterly direction into the bay from a point between Goodwick and Fishguard old town, together with two jetties each about 110 yards in length under the shelter of the breakwater. There was also to be extensive reclamation of the foreshore and railway connection to the two jetties. It was stated that the first and second breakwaters would together enclose a water area of 175 acres in which new ocean berths could be provided.

Following the successful initial handling of the Cunard liners, an announcement was made of the intention to deepen the water at the existing ocean quay to enable such vessels as the *Mauretania* to come alongside. For this purpose it was further announced that a powerful hopper barge was being hired from the Liverpool Port Authority.

Nothing further was heard of this venture and it is presumed that the rocky sea bed in the bay precluded dredging by conventional means to the full depth required.

Some work on the construction of the second breakwater was undertaken but clearly there were doubts over the suitability of the works authorised in 1908. Midway through 1912 it became known that advice had been obtained in the matter from Sir William Matthews, a noted civil engineer who specialised in dock and harbour work, and who was consulting engineer for Dover Harbour. His advice was that the breakwater would not have the effect of giving more shelter within the harbour, but would, in fact, make access thereto more difficult. At the half-yearly meeting of GWR shareholders in August 1912, the chairman stated that the scheme for building a large ocean quay had been postponed. By the end of the same year, it was clear that all idea of turning Fishguard into an Atlantic port had been given up, together with the completion of the works authorised in 1908.

The withdrawal of the Blue Funnel Line earlier in 1912 may have had some influence on these decisions but members of the GWR board, together with their opposite numbers in Ireland, cannot have been blind to the major developments which had been taking place at Southampton. These included deep-water berths suitable for the latest giants on the Atlantic scene, the White Star liners *Olympic* and *Titanic*. The prospect of now building a port at Fishguard which could compete effectively with Southampton was certainly remote.

Application was made to parliament for power formally to abandon most of the works under the 1908 Act and the necessary Bill was deposited for the session of 1913. It included provision for alterations to the original breakwater which had suffered damage in storms. Because of obstruction by some Irish members who used the opportunity to protest over the conduct of the Great Southern company during a strike, the Bill was defeated at the second reading. It was re-introduced in 1914 and was safely guided through its several stages, in spite of a repetition of the protests of the previous year.

It was on 8th July 1914 that the Bill received the Royal Assent, barely a month before the outbreak of war. The ships of the Booth Line had given up their Fishguard call earlier in the year and the days were numbered before wartime conditions would put an end to the calls by Cunard. By the time transatlantic services resumed after the war, the Cunard company had transferred its base from Liverpool to Southampton, and it was from Southampton that the *Mauretania* sailed on its first post-war passenger crossing to New York in 1920. Fishguard was left with no more than the memories of the big ships, its service to Rosslare lately operated by a single vessel, and the partly-completed breakwater of 1908 extending purposeless into the bay.

One cannot conclude a review of the development of Fishguard without some mention of the Swansea District Lines. The South Wales Railway had been built with a climb of about two miles, mostly at 1 in 52, from Landore to Cockett; as most passenger trains to New Milford, and later Fishguard, stopped at Landore to make connections

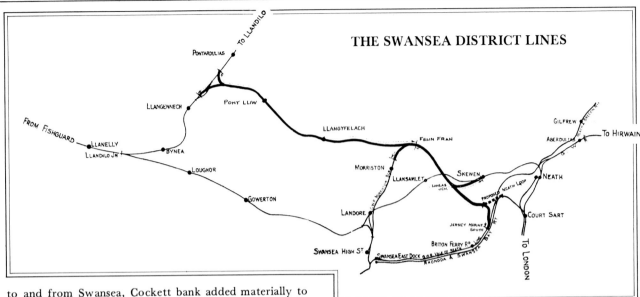

THE SWANSEA DISTRICT LINES

to and from Swansea, Cockett bank added materially to their schedules. Eastbound trains had a similar climb up to Cockett, commencing at Gowerton.

As a means of improving the flow of traffic to and from places west of Swansea, the GWR conceived the District Lines. Their principal feature was a new main line passing to the north of Swansea to give direct running between Neath and Llanelly; this line was laid out to leave the South Wales line at Skewen and to join the former Llanelly Railway at Llangennech, so to regain the South Wales at Llandilo Junction. About 3½ miles of the Llanelly Railway would thus become part of a main line and so would need to be doubled. The new main line was also to give an improved outlet for the Amman coalfield by means of a second junction with the Llanelly Railway, this time in the direction of Pontardulais. Additionally all goods traffic from the Llanelly area, not least of all the valuable output from the anthracite mines, was to be given improved access to Swansea Docks by means of a connection to the former Vale of Neath Railway, this being the section from Lonlas Junction, near Skewen, to Jersey Marine South. Finally there was to be an extension of the existing branch to Morriston to join the new main line at Felin Fran.

All the lines just mentioned were duly built, as also were links with the lines of the Rhondda & Swansea Bay Railway, which enabled long-distance trains using the Swansea District Main Line to avoid Neath as well, passing to and from the South Wales line at Court Sart Junction between Neath and Briton Ferry. It is these links which are used today (1987), the short section of the District Lines between Skewen and Lonlas Junction having been lifted.

Like the new line from Wootton Bassett to Patchway, the Swansea District Main Line was laid out as a fast through route, with a summit at Llangyfelach approached mainly at 1 in 120 for some three miles from the east, and for 4½ miles from the west. These gradients are certainly steeper than the 1 in 150 which seems to have been regarded by the GWR at the time as the desirable

maximum for its new main lines, but nevertheless they are very much easier than those at Cockett. The main engineering features are Llangyfelach Tunnel, 1,958 yards on the eastern approach to the summit, Penllergar Tunnel, 280 yards on the western approach, Lonlas Tunnel, 924 yards under the original South Wales line near Skewen, and the viaduct over the River Loughor, 220 yards in length with 11 masonry arches. Extensive yards were opened at Felin Fran, mainly to receive coal from new lines being built in the Clydach Valley, also a part of the Swansea District scheme.

There were delays in construction caused by labour troubles, as well as from unexpected engineering difficulties, not least of all in obtaining a firm foundation for the bridge over the River Tawe near Felin Fran. It was, therefore, not until 14th July 1913 that the main line could be opened for all classes of traffic throughout, almost nine years after its parliamentary authorisation. It had been used for coal traffic for some weeks prior to its general opening. There were two local stations, at Llangyfelach and at Pont Lliw, both built with four running lines through them. They were brought into use immediately for local goods traffic but it was not until 1 October 1923 that passengers were catered for. An infrequent service of rail-motors was then introduced between Swansea and Pontardulais via Morriston and Felin Fran (reverse). This service was not a success and it was withdrawn from 22nd September 1924, leaving the two stations as contenders for the record of short life for passenger operation.

The opening of the Swansea District Lines must have brought a sigh of relief to members of the operating and engineering staff, making available as it did an alternative route for places further west. In 1899 there had been a fall in Cockett Tunnel, following the removal of water from flooded coal workings beneath the line, and the tunnel had been closed to all traffic for about a month. Repairs were hurried through to permit the passage of goods trains, but passengers had to be taken over the

LNWR between Swansea (Victoria) and Gowerton for rather longer.

Conditions for the Swansea passenger were also improved in 1906 by the opening of a new connection at Landore. Although both steep and sharply curved, it permitted trains to run through between the company's principal station at High Street, and places in West Wales, thereby largely eliminating the irritating delays caused by the need to change trains at that disagreeable junction.

The use of lines of the Rhondda & Swansea Bay company in association with the Swansea District Lines, had been facilitated by an agreement made with that company in 1906. In return for a guaranteed income to its shareholders, the Rhondda company granted running powers to the GWR over the whole of its system. Between Neath and Swansea the lines of the two companies ran side by side to reach the docks at Swansea with their important facilities for the shipment of coal, and the agreement provided for the two companies to share the use of their respective coal tips. The arrangement effectively led to a four-line track becoming available between Neath and the Swansea Docks, a facility which must have been of assistance to the GWR in bringing traffic over the connection between Lonlas Junction and Jersey Marine when this was brought into use.

The hold of the GWR over so much of the coal traffic of South Wales was increased by the completion of a similar agreement with the Port Talbot Railway & Dock Company in 1907, although the docks remained in the control of the owning company. The Port Talbot company in its turn had entered into a like agreement with the South Wales Mineral Railway Company, so that the latter effectively also passed into the control of the GWR. The three companies maintained their legal independence until formal merger with the GWR under the Amalgamation Act of 1921.

Another scene in May 1911 with passengers from Boston freshly arrived at Paddington. The horse-drawn cabs are a study in themselves.

BBC Hulton Picture Library

4–4–0 locomotive No. 3387 *Roberts* leaving Kennaway tunnel near Dawlish in 1904. The doubling of this section of the line was one of the works completed in 1905. The third vehicle in the train is a new 'Dreadnought' dining car.

L & GRP, cty. David & Charles

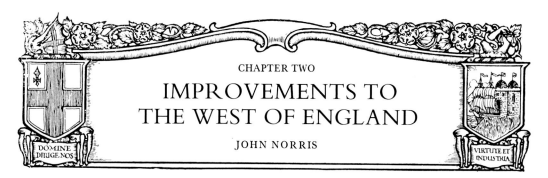

CHAPTER TWO

IMPROVEMENTS TO THE WEST OF ENGLAND

JOHN NORRIS

AS has been noted already, all trains at the beginning of the century between Paddington and the West of England were routed via Bath and Bristol. The avoiding line at Bristol, from East Depot to Pylle Hill, was already available for trains not needing to pass through Temple Meads station, but it was little used for passenger purposes because of the connections traditionally made in Bristol. The non-stop run between Paddington and Exeter was, however, being performed daily in each direction during the summer season. In 1900 it was undertaken only by the Newquay & Falmouth Corridor Express, which covered the 194 miles in 223 minutes in the down direction, ten minutes longer on the up journey. These runs were claimed as a world record for non-stop rail travel, but they were improved upon in July 1904 when the 'Cornish Riviera Limited' was introduced, again for the summer season only, running non-stop in each direction between Paddington and Plymouth (North Road), a distance of 246 miles to be covered in 265 minutes up, and two minutes longer in the down direction. The fact that trains could pass Exeter without stopping for water followed from the installation of the troughs at Exminster.

In addition to the increased facilities needed for holiday travel to the resorts of Devon and Cornwall, there was demand by shipping companies for fast trains to connect with the growing number of big ships, which called at Plymouth on their way to and from ports on the mainland of Europe. For the most part the sea-borne traffic was inward, with passengers and mails landed by tender from the liners which dropped anchor in Plymouth Sound. Some of the outward traffic called for special trains, however, and towards the end of 1899 it was announced that a train would run from Paddington to Plymouth every Tuesday morning to connect with the sailings of the Hamburg-Amerika Line. This train stopped at Exeter, where engines were changed, and again at Plymouth (Millbay) for dock engines to take over to work the train to the quay. On the first run, made on 24th October, it was stated that Exeter was reached in 218 minutes from Paddington.

The GWR had the contract for carrying the mails landed at Plymouth but the LSWR was free to compete for passengers, and in 1904 that company entered into a contract with the American Line to operate boat specials to Waterloo. The contract went into effect on 9th April of that year when a special train was run for passengers from the S.S. *St. Louis*. The LSWR had its own tenders

for use at Plymouth, and a separate terminal at Stonehouse Pool.

Most of the remaining passenger traffic passing through the port of Plymouth was still handled by the GWR so that the LSWR had much to compete for. But the LSWR trains had still to pass through St. David's station at Exeter, and the GWR had no scruples in exercising the right which it claimed to stop all LSWR trains in St. David's. While the stop by a boat special would have been for a few seconds only, psychologically the seconds counted for more as the LSWR trains had to tackle the climb of 1 in 37 up to their station at Queen Street from a standing start; had the stop not been made, they would, of course, have needed to pass through St. David's at a greatly reduced speed.

It was probably the loss of the mail contract which the GWR feared most, and the company made astonishing efforts to reduce the time taken by its ocean mail specials. Reports of the running of these trains have been quoted on many occasions. Suffice it now to say that on 9th April 1904, when the passengers from the *St. Louis* were taken to Waterloo under the new contract with the LSWR, a time of 262 minutes was recorded for the train carrying the mails from the same ship from Millbay Docks to Paddington; just three weeks later, on 30th April, with mails from the S.S. *Philadelphia* also of the American Line, the time was under four hours at 234 minutes, and then on 9th May it was 227 minutes by a train carrying mails landed from the S.S. *Kronprinz Wilhelm* of the North German Lloyd Line. This last-mentioned run stands as one of the most famous pieces of railway history, when a top speed of 102.3 m.p.h. was attributed to the celebrated locomotive *City of Truro* while descending Wellington bank towards Taunton, the first time an authoritative claim had been made for a speed of 100 m.p.h. by a steam locomotive.

The remarkable performance of *City of Truro* seems to have caused concern to GWR management as to possible adverse public reaction to travel at such speeds, and several years elapsed before the claim to the speed record became general knowledge, although an abridged log of the run appeared in the *Great Western Railway Magazine* in the month after it occurred. Although much fine running by GWR locomotives was to figure in the railway press over the years, not least of all in the era of the 'Cheltenham Flyer', it was not until 1939 that a speed of 100 m.p.h. was claimed again for the company. It was

Witham station looking towards Frome.
Collection R. S. Carpenter

then attributed to the locomotive *Builth Castle*, while descending Honeybourne bank with a down Worcester express.

Without minimising the achievements in working the ocean mail trains, it has to be acknowledged that the loadings were light. Five bogie vans would have been typical from Plymouth, with one, or perhaps two of them detached at Bristol. The stop to detach was sometimes made in Temple Meads station, and the train might then continue its journey to Paddington by way of the new line through Badminton. If, however, the original route to Paddington via Bath was to be used, the stop was more likely to have been made at Pylle Hill, and the train would then have taken the Bristol avoiding line. At the time of the record runs of 1904 it was also the practice to change engines at Bristol. In later years it became normal for the mail specials to run non-stop from Plymouth to Paddington, the portion for Bristol being slipped at Bedminster.

Even with these light trains, the locomotives required careful handling west of Bristol to safeguard their water supplies. Unless a driver adopted the unwelcome course of making an additional stop for water at Exeter, he had a run of nearly 90 miles from Plymouth before he was able to replenish his supply from the troughs at Creech, and this run included the formidable Hemerdon bank. Reflecting now on the situation, it is ironic that these trains should just have missed the benefit of the troughs at Exminster, as some of the logs mention slacks for engineering work near Starcross, which was evidently in connection with the laying of these troughs in readiness for the introduction of the 'Cornish Riviera Limited'.

However, it was largely for passenger traffic that a new main line to the West Country was needed, and its development was another example of the way the GWR was able to make better use of its existing lines by a process of upgrading, and the building of new connecting lines between them. Before the new lines were completed, the districts concerned were served by lines, some of which had their origins early in the company's history. There was the Wilts, Somerset & Weymouth Railway from

Thingley Junction on the original main line west of Chippenham, passing through Westbury, Frome, Castle Cary, Yeovil, and Dorchester; between Dorchester and Weymouth it was joint with the LSWR, the whole dating from the years 1848-1857. Even earlier there was the Berks & Hants line from Reading to Hungerford, dating from 1847, while the Berks & Hants Extension had been opened in 1862 from Hungerford to Devizes where it met the branch of 1857 from Holt Junction on the Wilts, Somerset & Weymouth Railway.

Further west, the Bristol & Exeter Railway had opened a branch to Yeovil in 1853, leaving its main line at Durston, about six miles east of Taunton. This originally terminated at Hendford station in Yeovil, but it had been extended to connect with the Wilts, Somerset & Weymouth at Yeovil, Pen Mill. At the start of the century the branch was single line, as was also that from Hungerford to Devizes and Holt Junction.

The idea of a direct line to the West Country had been very much in Brunel's mind. In 1847 he spoke of the Berks & Hants line becoming in all probability the main line to the West Country. Much was happening in the field of railway politics at that time which would have made this seem likely, but many of the lines then being projected were not built so that nearly sixty years were to elapse before Brunel's foresight became a reality. The idea had not been allowed to die completely, however, as parliamentary powers for new lines, very much as ultimately built, had been obtained in 1883, and had been renewed or modified from time to time.

The first part of the works on the new line to the West Country was that between Hungerford and Westbury, commenced in 1897. The Berks & Hants Extension was utilised for about 19½ miles from Hungerford to the point at which a new station was built, named Patney & Chirton, the existing single line being doubled, many of the curves and gradients considerably eased, bridges reconstructed, and platforms lengthened at the existing stations. From Patney to Westbury a conventional double line of railway was built, having two intermediate stations — at Lavington and at Edington & Bratton. The length of new line was about 14½ miles, for about half of which there was a falling gradient of 1 in 222 commencing immediately on leaving Patney, and it was then level for the remainder of the distance to Westbury. The minimum radius of a curve was 60 chains, while the only engineering structure of note was Lavington viaduct, 120 yards long with eight arches.

Goods traffic commenced over the new section on 29th July 1900, followed by a service of four purely local passenger trains each way on 1st October of the same year. Three of the passenger trains ran between Westbury and Patney only, the fourth between Westbury and Woodborough.

A service of three fast passenger trains between Paddington and Weymouth was introduced on 1st July 1901, the best time being 220 minutes, both up and down, for the 154½ miles. Although the distance was still nearly twelve miles further than by the LSWR from Waterloo, the GWR could provide competitive times to both Dorchester and Weymouth. In the case of Yeovil, London passengers had generally to change at Yeovil Junction by the LSWR, so the GWR was able to offer them savings in time of up to 16 minutes. Of the three down trains, two slipped a portion at Newbury, and two at Patney for the Devizes line.

From Westbury the Wilts, Somerset & Weymouth Railway ran in roughly a south-westerly direction, following the valleys of two small rivers, the Frome and then the Brue, until it reached Castle Cary where it took a more southerly course towards Yeovil. It was, therefore, at Castle Cary that the next section of new line commenced in order to fill the gap of 15½ miles to a point west of Langport, where it joined the Yeovil branch of the former Bristol & Exeter Railway. The point where the two joined was named Curry Rivel Junction, after a village two miles away. From here it was about 6½ miles to the Bristol & Exeter main line at Durston, but there was a sharp curve on the approach by the branch to Durston station, so that a further piece of new line was built in the form of a cut-off nearly three miles in length, from the station on the branch at Athelney to a new junction with the Bristol & Exeter line at Cogload. The works west of Castle Cary were commenced in 1903.

For the first seven miles from Castle Cary to Charlton Mackrell, the new line contained no engineering features of comment, except to say that it included very little curvature, and a length of perfectly straight line extending for 2½ miles. To minimise tunnelling it then took a loop to the north, passing through the village of Somerton, and at Long Sutton & Pitney it resumed a virtually straight course for the remaining three miles through Langport to Curry Rivel Junction. It was still necessary to build Somerton tunnel, 1,053 yards, and Somerton viaduct with five arches over the valley of the River Cary.

On leaving Langport, the line passed into a stretch of country which had been beset by flooding over the centuries, and which was accordingly a notorious area for railway construction. Drained by the River Parrett towards Bridgwater, much of it is only around 20 feet above sea level, and some is even below sea level. When

Bridge over the railway near junction at Castle Cary showing in the distance the Weymouth express. The new line towards Langport curved to the right just beyond the bridge.

Cty. Railway Gazette

Building viaduct over the River Cary at Somerton.

Cty. Railway Gazette

the branch from Durston to Yeovil was built, the track had not been raised sufficiently high above ground level, so that flooding had been a constant problem. Between Langport and Curry Rivel Junction it was possible to plan accordingly from the start — firstly a viaduct was built having ten spans each of 55 feet, followed to the west by a bridge of 105 feet over the River Parrett with two approach arches on either side, each having a span of nearly 40 feet. It was necessary to excavate to a depth of no less than 50 feet into the peat before a firm base was reached on which to build the foundations for these works.

From Curry Rivel Junction to Athelney the original line was completely rebuilt, being raised well above flood level, and, of course, it was doubled. The rebuilding

Construction in progress at Keinton Mandeville.   *Lens of Sutton*

included the provision of numerous new arches to facilitate
the passage of flood waters, and to obtain adequate foundations for these arches, the piling had again to be driven
up to 50 feet into the soft ground. Similar difficulties had
to be faced in building the Durston cut-off. The old level
of the line may still be seen in places from a passing train.

Conventional turn-outs were laid at Castle Cary and
Cogload, but in 1931 the layout at Cogload was altered to
provide a fly-over for trains approaching the junction
from the Bristol direction. In association with this change
the point of junction between the Bristol and the Westbury lines was moved to Creech, two miles nearer
Taunton. Between Westbury and Castle Cary the line was
already double, and required little alteration. The cut-offs
for Westbury and Frome were completed in 1932.

The layout at Westbury was completely remodelled
and a new passenger station was built there, having two
long island platforms to facilitate interchange between
trains. Much of the work at Westbury was complete in
time for the opening of the line from Patney. The only
other station to be extensively altered in association with
the improvements was that at Newbury. Here, the alterations included the provision of four tracks through the
station, together with completely new buildings which
were brought into use in April 1909.

West of Castle Cary the first section of the new line to
be opened was from that place to Charlton Mackrell. This
became available for all traffic on 1st July 1905, passengers
being catered for by a service of five trips by railmotor.
The remainder of the new works were brought into use in
short sections for goods traffic only and were complete
throughout by the end of May 1906. Through passenger

Construction in progress at Somerton.   *Lens of Sutton*

trains, and a passenger service to the remaining local
stations, did not commence until the introduction of the
summer timetables on 2nd July following. In spite of the
cut-off at Durston, some local trains continued to operate
over the old line to make connections at Durston station.

A special train for the press and other guests was run
over the new route from Paddington to Plymouth on
Friday, 29th June. Always quick to seize an opportunity
to publicise its facilities, the company was able to include
among its guests on the train a group of German journalists
who left Plymouth the same evening on board the North
German Lloyd liner, the S.S. *Bremen*.

The full summer service did not become operative until
21st July when the 'Cornish Riviera Limited' was reintro-
duced, once more running non-stop between Paddington

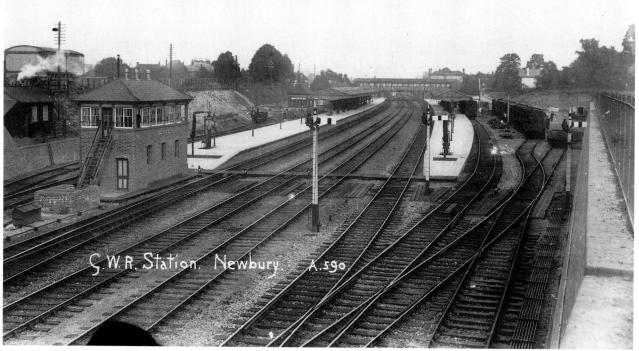

Top: Newbury station, looking east, before rebuilding. *Bottom:* As rebuilt, the bay on the right was used mainly by trains for Winchester and Southampton, while trains for the Lambourn Valley used the bay on the left.

Museum of English Rural Life

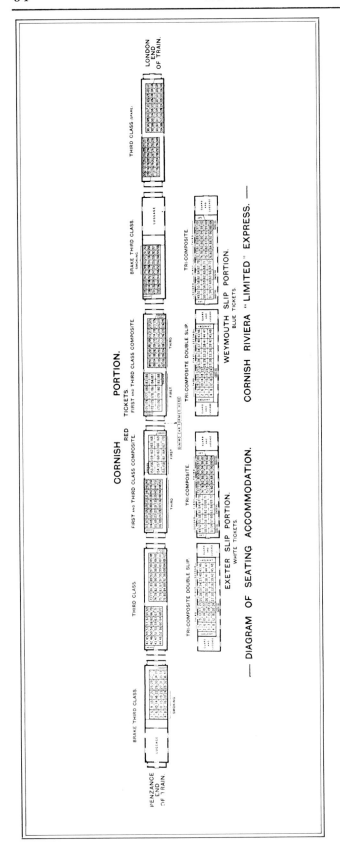

PENZANCE END OF TRAIN.

BRAKE THIRD CLASS

THIRD CLASS

CORNISH PORTION.

RED TICKETS.
FIRST AND THIRD CLASS COMPOSITE

BRAKE THIRD CLASS

LONDON END OF TRAIN.

THIRD CLASS (SPARE).

TRI-COMPOSITE DOUBLE SLIP

EXETER SLIP PORTION.
WHITE TICKETS

TRI-COMPOSITE

TRI-COMPOSITE

TRI-COMPOSITE DOUBLE SLIP

WEYMOUTH SLIP PORTION.
BLUE TICKETS

TRI-COMPOSITE

— DIAGRAM OF SEATING ACCOMMODATION.   CORNISH RIVIERA "LIMITED" EXPRESS. —

and Plymouth. The journey time for this run was now 250 minutes, and although the distance had been reduced by about twenty miles compared with the route via Bristol, it was still claimed as a world record for a non-stop run. Male and female attendants travelled on the train to look after invalids and children.

At this time the 'Cornish Riviera Limited' comprised a ten-coach formation from Paddington, six coaches going through to Penzance, with two slipped at Westbury, and two more slipped at Exeter. The portion for Penzance included a restaurant car. Following the procedure adopted in the previous year, a reservation system was available for all seats on the train. The practice of slipping coaches from trains to the West Country continued for many years. Quite apart from providing an improved service to many places, slip coaches were of some operational assistance in that train loads could be reduced, without stopping to detach, before severe gradients were encountered such as those at Wellington and Rattery. The slip at Westbury from this train normally went through to Weymouth, and was described in Bradshaw at one time as the 'Weymouth Limited Express'.

Of the other trains using the new route, two in the down direction were booked to run non-stop from Paddington to Exeter, 173 miles. In the one case the time was 185 minutes, in the other it was three minutes longer.

While the opening of its shorter route to the West Country on 2nd July 1906 was an undoubted triumph for the GWR, the event was overshadowed by the disaster which had overtaken a special boat express from Plymouth by the LSWR route at Salisbury in the early hours of the previous day. Twenty-eight people died in the crash, including twenty-four passengers off the S.S. *New York* of the American Line. Although the GWR would now be able to operate boat specials over its shorter route through Westbury, and it was admitted that there was keen competition between the two companies at the time, the inquiry into the disaster found no truth in statements that passengers by the boat trains made a practice of tipping drivers to put up fast times, or that the LSWR encouraged record breaking. The crash was attributed to tragic human error.

It may well be that competition between the GWR and LSWR for ocean liner traffic at Plymouth was never quite the same again. In 1910, following protracted negotiations on many points on which the two companies might work together more closely, they entered into a working agreement, one consequence of which was the withdrawal of the LSWR from the liner traffic at Plymouth. In view of the growth of Southampton as a port, the LSWR may well have felt that it had little to lose by so doing.

It is of interest also to consider briefly the economies of working the boat specials. On the fatal night at Salisbury, the train was carrying just 48 passengers, admittedly all first-class. In an interview published in the *Railway Magazine*, a GWR official stated that his company would run a special train from Millbay Docks to Paddington for 25 first-class passengers, or the equivalent in fares. The latter represented a total receipt of rather less than £40. It seems impossible to believe now that such a sum could have met the costs of the train. Not having the mail

A train of 'Dreadnought' coaches, probably the 'Limited'.
A. R. Kingdon

contract, the LSWR might well have been cutting its losses by giving up the ocean liner traffic at Plymouth.

When the LSWR withdrew, the GWR purchased its principal tender, the S.S. *Atalanta*, a modern vessel built as recently as 1907, and shortly afterwards it was reported on similar duties at Fishguard. The GWR had its own tenders at Plymouth, although it also used for the purpose from time to time spare vessels from its service between Weymouth and the Channel Islands. In 1908 the GWR obtained two purpose-built tenders, respectively *Sir Francis Drake* and *Sir Walter Raleigh*. Although both were intended for service at Plymouth, the latter was in attendance at Fishguard for the first call by the *Mauretania* in August of that year.

The Cornish Riviera Express waiting to leave No. 1 platform at Paddington in 1912.

BBC Hulton Picture Library

British Railways

A viaduct under construction between Acton and High Wycombe.

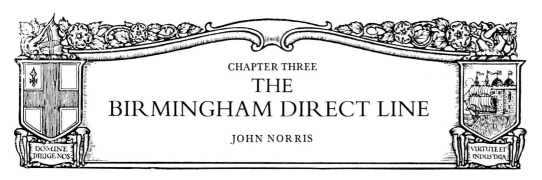

CHAPTER THREE

THE
BIRMINGHAM DIRECT LINE

JOHN NORRIS

BY the end of the eighteenth century, Birmingham had gone a long way to establishing itself as the industrial capital of the West Midlands, although it was not until 1838 that it obtained its charters of incorporation. In the same year the London & Birmingham Railway was opened throughout. In contrast, the GWR was late in reaching this important centre of industry and trade, and it was not until 1st October 1852 that the company opened its station at Snow Hill upon the inauguration of a broad gauge service from Paddington via Oxford. Nine years later to the day, the company made history again when a train left Paddington for the first time on the standard gauge; bound for Birmingham and beyond, it also introduced through services from Paddington to Chester and Birkenhead.

By the closing years of the century, corridor coaches were in use on the principal trains on the Birmingham line, although it appears to have been the summer of 1904 before the facility of a restaurant car was introduced, going down on a train at 11.25 a.m. from Paddington as far as Shrewsbury, and leaving there on its return journey at 5.45 p.m. In the summer of 1896, one train in each direction was scheduled to run non-stop between Paddington and Leamington, following the installation of the water troughs at Goring in the previous autumn, and in the summer of 1898 non-stop running was introduced between Paddington and Birmingham, presumably made possible by the laying of the water troughs at Rowington, between Hatton and Kingswood (now Lapworth). The initial non-stop schedule between Paddington and Snow Hill was 147 minutes for the 129¼ miles, but by 1904 this had been reduced to 137 minutes. Additional water troughs were brought into use in 1906 at Adderbury, between Aynho and King's Sutton.

With these improvements, the company was able actively to compete for American traffic passing through the port of Liverpool, and, indeed, had an office in New York. In 1894 advertisements in an American travel guide reminded the reader that 'Passengers should be careful to ask for Great Western tickets'. With this expanding outlook, it is perhaps not surprising that ocean liner specials were run between Paddington and Birkenhead; such a special in 1905 covered the 229 miles in 258 minutes, stopping only at Wolverhampton to change engines.

Throughout the second half of the nineteenth century the population of Birmingham had been growing, reaching 478,000 at the census of 1891. Twenty years later, following the absorption of such surrounding areas as Aston Manor (until then a borough in its own right), and what had been administratively the rural districts of Handsworth, Erdington, Kings Norton, Yardley and Quinton, the population of the enlarged city was 840,000, and was still increasing. Greater Birmingham by then extended from Oscott in the north to Rubery and Rednal in the south.

To compete effectively with the LNWR for traffic to and from the Midlands, as well as the districts served from Shrewsbury and Chester, the GWR needed an improved and shortened route between Paddington and Birmingham. The first positive steps for such a route had culminated with the grant of powers by parliament in 1897 for a new line, 23 miles in length, from the main line outside Paddington, at a point which became known as Old Oak Common Junction, to the former Wycombe Railway at High Wycombe, passing by way of Denham, Gerrards Cross, and Beaconsfield. The Wycombe Railway had been opened in stages between 1854 and 1864, from the GWR at Maidenhead, through High Wycombe and Princes Risborough, to rejoin the GWR at Kennington Junction outside Oxford; there was also a branch from Princes Risborough to Aylesbury. Completion of the new line to High Wycombe would thus give a new route between Paddington and Oxford, a distance of 55¾ miles or about 8 miles less than the company's only other route via Reading.

It was clearly the intention of the GWR to develop this shorter route between Paddington and Oxford for through traffic because powers were obtained in 1900 to carry out substantial improvements between Princes Risborough and Kennington Junction. These comprised a new line of 5½ miles in length to avoid the tunnel near Wheatley, together with alterations in the levels, and the widening for double track, of the remaining 13 miles.

In the meantime the GCR had appeared on the scene, and, being dissatisfied with the outcome of the arrangements which it had made with the Metropolitan Railway for a joint line from Quainton Road for most of the way into London, had become involved in discussions with the GWR. The result was the creation of a joint committee of the two companies, recognised by parliament in 1899, with power to construct a line from the GCR at Grendon Underwood to the GWR at Princes Risborough, a distance of about 15 miles. The existing single line of the GWR between Princes Risborough and High Wycombe was to

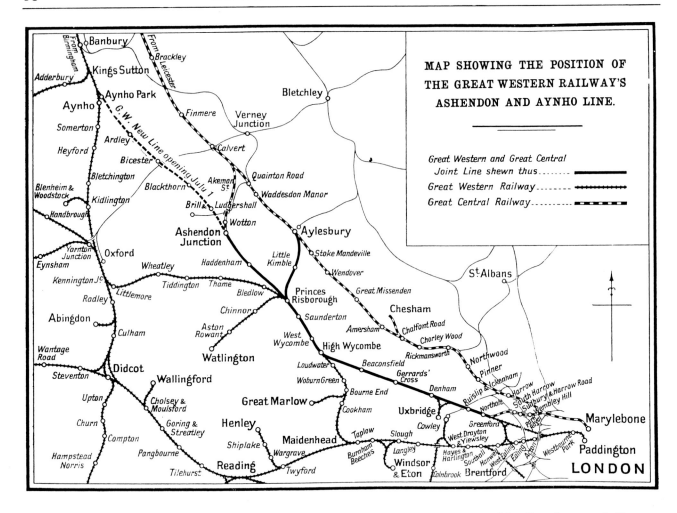

MAP SHOWING THE POSITION OF THE GREAT WESTERN RAILWAY'S ASHENDON AND AYNHO LINE.

Great Western and Great Central Joint Line shewn thus.........
Great Western Railway..........
Great Central Railway..........

be sold to the joint committee for the sum of £225,000, and was to be widened for double track, while the powers for building the new line from Old Oak Common, as between Northolt and High Wycombe, were to be vested in the joint committee. Under separate powers the GCR was to build a line between Northolt and a point on its own London Extension at Neasden, so still obtaining access to Marylebone.

At this time the GWR and the GCR were on the most cordial terms, and on 20th March 1899 the GCR commenced working goods and coal trains with its own locomotives over the GWR through to West London Junction outside Paddington, their route from Aylesbury being by way of Princes Risborough, High Wycombe, and Maidenhead. A timetable for December 1899 shows a weekday service of five such trains. The arrangement was rendered unnecessary when the GCR line between Woodford and Banbury was brought into use on 1st June 1900.

Such was the relationship with the GCR that at the half-yearly general meeting of the GWR in February 1902, a shareholder asked whether there were any foundation for reports that the company was to acquire the GCR. There was certainly every reason for the two companies to be on very friendly terms. To be able to share the cost of

the construction of some 35 miles of new main line was for each a major consideration, and, in the circumstances, the GWR could have been well-satisfied over the disposal of the section of the line between Princes Risborough and High Wycombe.

However, it was probably the GCR which had the greater reason to be thankful for the arrangements. It had been finding difficulty in raising finance for the several other major schemes which it had in hand, and its directors must have felt great relief by the undertaking of the GWR to provide the whole of the finance in the first instance from its substantial resources to build the joint line. A meeting of GWR shareholders in 1907 was told that the GCR had been paying interest on half of the expenditure at the rate of 4% per annum. This had, in fact, applied only since the opening of the joint line for traffic, prior to which date interest had been a capital charge on the joint committee. It may be noted that the GWR had also provided the capital for the construction of the line between Woodford and Banbury.

The plans for the improvement of the line between Princes Risborough and Oxford were not proceeded with, and it seems likely that the GWR directors realised that the interests of their company would be better served by a completely new line in the direction of Birmingham, thus avoiding Oxford entirely. This was the line through Bicester from Ashendon, where it would leave the joint line towards Grendon Underwood, to join the original line to Birmingham at Aynho. Plans for such a line went ahead, and the necessary powers were obtained from parliament in 1905. The further length of new line now to be constructed was a little over 18 miles.

There remained the question of regularising some of the arrangements between the GWR and the GCR over the joint line. Although the section between Ashendon and Grendon Underwood had been initiated as part of the joint undertaking, the GWR had no direct interest in it, and it was accordingly taken over by the GCR with effect from 26th July 1907, that company reimbursing the GWR for the costs it had incurred towards the construction. At the same time, the GCR had no rights over the line between Princes Risborough and Aylesbury, and so this was transferred to the joint committee, together with the interest of the GWR in the joint station at Aylesbury. For these transfers the GWR was to receive £82,000 from the joint committee. Their effective date was 1st July 1907.

As regards a financial settlement, it was agreed by the two companies to issue £2,500,000 of 3½% loan stock under their joint and several guarantees, out of which the GWR would be reimbursed for its expenditure on the new lines remaining in the control of the joint committee, and

for the two pieces of line transferred to the committee. The issue of the stock was advertised in January 1908, and successfully completed, so that at their half-yearly meeting in the following August, GWR shareholders were told that £1,864,200 had been received out of the issue as recoupment of the capital provided for the purposes of the joint undertaking.

Like the South Wales Direct Line, the construction works were on the grand scale, both for the section which was for the joint undertaking and that which was to be the property of the GWR alone. Four tracks were built from the junction at Northolt to the station at Ruislip & Ickenham (now West Ruislip), and four tracks were also provided through the stations at Greenford, Denham, Gerrards Cross, and Beaconsfield. At High Wycombe and Princes Risborough the existing stations were rebuilt with four lines through each.

Doubling of the existing line between High Wycombe and Princes Risborough entailed the building of a new viaduct through the centre of High Wycombe, the old single-line viaduct still standing alongside it in 1987. The other major work on the doubling was the construction of a completely new up line on an easier gradient for about two miles between Princes Risborough and Saunderton, a great benefit for all traffic passing towards London but particularly for the heavy coal trains which were to be worked that way by the GCR. Saunderton station was left

A cutting being made near the site of one of the stations between Acton and High Wycombe. The structure of the drainage work is clearly demonstrated.   *British Railways*

In this scene at Denham a single line suffices for the contractors but the platforms are already prepared for the four tracks which were to be laid between them.
Lens of Sutton

Bridges near Brill, with Brill tunnel in the background. The iron girder bridge carried the Brill Tramway over the line.
Cty. Railway Gazette

Finishing touches are put to the new station at Bicester.   *Cty. Railway Gazette*

largely unaltered, already having double track for crossing purposes on the single line. The station at West Wycombe, not a crossing place, was rebuilt to allow for the installation of four tracks, although the centre through lines were never laid. Elsewhere, the alignment of the old single line may be seen in several places, one notable survival being at the bridge which carries the railway over the road from High Wycombe to Aylesbury, about midway between West Wycombe and Saunderton. Between Princes Risborough and Aynho, four lines were laid through the stations at Haddenham, Brill & Ludgershall, Bicester, and Ardley.

Although there were several short viaducts between Northolt and High Wycombe, also White House tunnel of 348 yards to the west of Beaconsfield, the main structural works were at the north end of the line. These were Ardley (or Fritwell) tunnel, 1,147 yards, and the two Souldern viaducts, respectively 18 arches and 330 yards in length, and 24 arches and 400 yards in length. Water troughs were installed about half-a-mile west of Ruislip & Ickenham station.

To the observer there could hardly have been a better place to appreciate the grand scale of the work than from the road over the line at the end of Gerrards Cross station, there to admire the spaciousness of the station layout, and to look along the straight line disappearing into the distance towards Beaconsfield. There were other long straight stretches — more than four miles between Princes Risborough and Haddenham, and three lengths each of more than two miles between Haddenham and Aynho — and locomotive crews were well able to use these straight stretches to their best advantage as there was little curvature between to inhibit them. Over junctions the minimum radius was half-a-mile, and on open track a

minimum radius of one mile between Northolt and High Wycombe, even two miles north of Princes Risborough.

A feature of the layout at junctions was the adoption of fly-overs to avoid delays caused by conflicting movements of trains. At Northolt, down trains from Marylebone were carried under the GWR lines before entering the joint section, while at Ashendon GWR up trains were carried over the GCR which took a more northerly course towards Grendon Underwood. Similarly at Aynho down trains from the direction of Bicester were carried over the original route from Oxford to join it on the down side. The approach to the fly-over at Ashendon was on a gradient of 1 in 150 but there was no other adverse gradient as steep, a remarkable tribute to the skill with which the whole of the new works had been planned by the GWR engineers.

At some of the stations where four lines were laid, goods trains of up to 80 wagons, plus engine and brake van, could be held. If, as was normally the case, the points at either end of the platform were controlled from a single signal box, the loop would be too short to accommodate the whole of such a train, and so the problem was solved by building an extension siding at either end of the loop. When a heavy goods train needed to be held, it would run through the platform loop, into the facing siding as far as was necessary for the brake van to clear the points at the entrance to the loop. It would then set back into the trailing siding until the engine was clear of the points over which it would leave the loop to continue its journey. Among the places where arrangements of this nature were adopted were Brill & Ludgershall, Bicester and Ardley.

The stations throughout were built in red brick to what were largely standard GWR designs. An interesting variation was made at Gerrards Cross where the station

The station at Gerrards Cross, described as being 'for the Chalfonts', shortly after it was opened. *Lens of Sutton*

Steam railmotor No. 98 at Gerrards Cross on a service to Westbourne Park. *British Railways*

A train for Paddington entering Beaconsfield in 1912.   *British Railways*

The same train calling at Beaconsfield on its way to High Wycombe. The three tail lamps were a requirement which lasted into the 1930s.
British Railways

was in a cutting and it was not practicable to provide road access at platform level. Here, effectively, the standard type of single-storey building, as is found at Beaconsfield for example, was divided into two halves placed one above the other. The largest new station to be built was that at Bicester. Apart from being a town of some market and commercial importance, it is the centre for what was popular hunting country. The station was accordingly provided with refreshment facilities, together with changing rooms for passengers arriving to take part in the hunt.

The construction work for the joint undertaking was under the supervision of GWR engineers, although GCR staff later took charge on the section between Ashendon and Grendon Underwood. This portion was laid out in the same style as the remainder of the joint undertaking, and the two intermediate stations, at Wotton and at Akeman Street, each had four tracks through them, with platforms on the outer lines only. This feature is not common on the GCR, which generally preferred island platforms on its London Extension, although it was adopted by the company for the stations provided at Wembley Hill, Sudbury & Harrow Road, and South Harrow (later

Sudbury Hill), for the opening of the line between Neasden and Northolt. It is difficult to escape the conclusion that a strong GWR influence was at work when this piece of line was planned.

Although local traffic was being worked as far as Greenford from Paddington, both via Old Oak Common Junction and via the Greenford loop, before 1904 was out, traffic over the joint line did not commence until 20th November 1905 when both companies introduced through goods trains. In the case of the GWR these trains can only have been working via Princes Risborough, to and from Oxford or beyond. The joint line became fully operational for both the passenger and the goods traffic of the two companies on 2nd April 1906. Work on building the line from Ashendon to Aynho was then only about to start, so that goods traffic over it did not commence until 4th April 1910, followed by passenger services on 1st July of the same year.

The GWR now had a route from London to Birmingham of 110½ miles, 19 miles less than it had via Oxford, and 2 miles less than that of the LNWR from Euston, so that it was able to compete with the LNWR for traffic on equal terms. This competition meant express trains

The buildings on the down side at High Wycombe as seen from the approach road. This has been the site of the station for the town since 1864, the original station having been built as the terminus of the line from Maidenhead on a site to the right of that shown.

British Railways

Two scenes on the Birmingham direct line in 1912. The top is a reminder of the joint interest in the section nearer London as a Great Central goods train passes Ickenham (now West Ruislip). Below, a Great Western passenger train is seen near Northolt.

Collection R. C. Riley

A rural scene at Greenford station.   *Lens of Sutton*

Down Birkenhead express passing Old Oak Common in 1912. The locomotive is No. 4005 *Polar Star*, and the train comprises four 57 ft
coaches with a 70 ft dining car in the middle, all in crimson lake livery.   *Collection R. C. Riley*

between Paddington and Birmingham, non-stop in two
hours, and such trains were introduced immediately on
the opening of the Bicester route for passenger traffic.
The LNWR had introduced trains non-stop in two hours
between Euston and Birmingham in 1902.

Initially five trains daily made the run from Paddington
in two hours, including one which stopped at High
Wycombe only. All served Leamington by slip coach, one
slipped also at Princes Risborough, one at Banbury, one
at Knowle, and one at both Banbury and Knowle; the
latter, the 4.00 p.m., thus left Paddington with three
separate slip coaches. The 11.05 a.m. from Paddington
made Birmingham its only stop before Shrewsbury. On
Mondays there was an additional train which called at
Ealing Broadway, and then made use of the Greenford
loop to run non-stop to Birmingham; this train was
allowed an additional five minutes for its journey, and it
did not have a slip portion.

In the reverse direction all trains stopped at Leamington
but only one was booked to Paddington in the even two
hours, an additional five minutes being allowed for the
five other principal trains. One of these trains stopped also
at Banbury, one at High Wycombe, and one at Ealing
Broadway, while one slipped a coach at Banbury.

Between High Wycombe and both Paddington and
Marylebone there was a rapid growth in the local traffic,
a total of some 25 trains operating on a normal weekday
in 1910. Between Ashendon and Aynho, however, the
line had a close similarity with the South Wales Direct
Line, passing through a district having but a small popu-

lation, with Bicester having traffic needs not unlike those
of Badminton.

Notwithstanding the availability at this time of four
down trains, and five up, between Euston and Birmingham, all non-stop in two hours, the new GWR service was
an instant success. In the summer of 1911 eight-coach
formations, hauled by 4–6–0 locomotives of the 'Saint'
class, were general out of Paddington on the two-hour
schedules. These loads had normally been reduced to five
coaches by the time Birmingham was reached by reason
of the slip workings. One reason for the slips at Leamington was the need to ease the work of the locomotive up
Hatton bank, away from the valley of the Warwickshire
Avon, and it was not until 1930 that slip working at
Leamington largely ceased. By then locomotives
of the 'King' class were fully established on the run, and
it was realised that Hatton bank was no longer the
obstacle it once had seemed. One consequence of the end
of slip working at Leamington was that there were fewer
through coaches from Paddington to Stratford-upon-Avon,
to which place the slip coaches had often worked forward
from the time of their inception.

To handle the increasing traffic, the GWR needed a
much enlarged central station in Birmingham. The station
at Snow Hill, as then existing, was the second on the site,
dating from 1871. It had two main platforms, with short
bays at the north end only, but pressure on operating
space was eased to some extent by the availability of four
tracks between the platforms. As these two platforms
each had a face of some 500 feet only, they were unable

to hold trains longer than seven of the 70 ft coaches which were becoming standard on main line services early in the present century. Certainly the GWR was looking ahead to a time when much longer trains would be usual, as well as to the need to handle an increased suburban traffic, and it accordingly embarked on a scheme for the enlargement of Snow Hill station and its approaches.

There were serious restrictions on the way the station could be enlarged; public thoroughfares ran on either side, while the rail approach from the south was through a tunnel. The main enlargement had, therefore, to be undertaken by extending the two platforms at their north end, so that they were ultimately 1200 ft in length, and so able to hold a train of seventeen of the latest coaches. Nonetheless, sufficient room was obtained for widening, and an additional running line was constructed to serve

the outer face of each platform. Two island platforms were thus created, having a maximum width of 88 ft, while at their north end two bay platforms were built on either side, those on the down side, which were used more for passenger purposes than those on the up side, accommodating comfortably the type of six-coach train which was to become normal on services such as those to Cardiff via Hereford.

The northward extensions took the platforms over Great Charles Street, from which a pedestrian entrance with booking office was provided. The main pedestrian entrance, however, was from Colmore Row, by means of an archway constructed through what had been the Great Western Hotel, and this led into a covered circulating area, on the opposite side of which was built a large booking office. Vehicular access to this area was given from Livery

A busy scene at Snow Hill, Birmingham, before the departure of an up express.   *British Railways*

Snow Hill station from the north, before rebuilding. *British Railways*

Snow Hill station from the north, after rebuilding. A local train, probably for Stourbridge or Wolverhampton, is standing in the bay to the right.
British Railways

Street on the west side. The way thence was along wide footways to a bridge, from which stairways led to the platforms.

Although the company was adopting a policy of operating its own hotel and refreshment services in the 1890s, and had taken over direct management of the Great Western Hotel at Paddington in 1896, the hotel at Birmingham had not been brought under the management of the company, doubtless because of the longer-term plans for the station. Most of the hotel building was turned into railway offices, but the ground floor was retained as a restaurant, managed by the company.

With the ground on either side of the station falling from south to north, indeed from well above rail level to well below, access was readily obtained from the streets on either side to docks for perishable traffic, as well as to basements for station stores and service areas. For passengers, however, surely few can have failed to be impressed by the sheer spaciousness of the structure. Extensive offices and refreshment rooms were built on the platforms,

Another view of Snow Hill station from the north, showing the long platforms available for main-line trains when the rebuilding had been completed.   *British Railways*

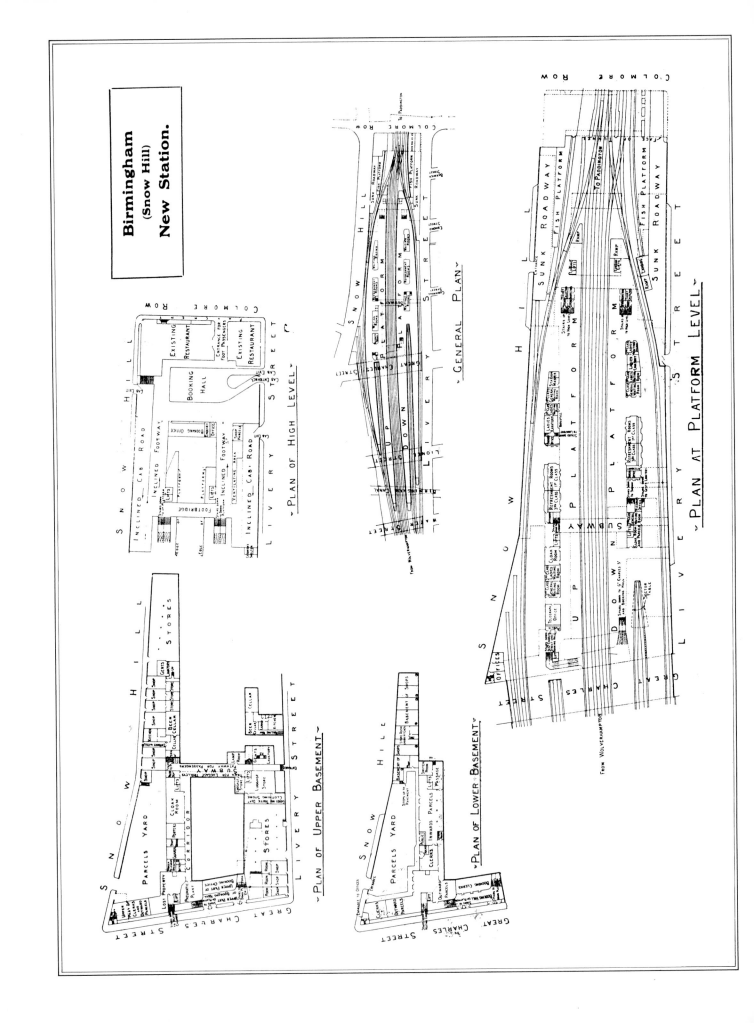

Birmingham (Snow Hill) New Station.

~ Plan of High Level ~

~ General Plan ~

~ Plan at Platform Level ~

~ Plan of Upper Basement ~

~ Plan of Lower Basement ~

View inside Snow Hill station in 1913, looking south. The principal access to the platforms was by stairs from the bridge at the far end of the station. On the left, almost beneath the clock, a sign indicates the luncheon room, additional to a refreshment room just beyond.
British Railways

Another view inside Snow Hill showing No. 11 platform with No. 7 platform to the left. In later years No. 11 platform was largely used by stopping trains for the Leamington line.
British Railways

SIGNALLING AT SNOW HILL STATION, BIRMINGHAM.

Exterior of North Box.

Interior of North Box.

Facing point layout, South Box.

Facing point layout, North Box.

Mechanism for semaphores.

Double dwarf signal.

Illuminated shaft route indicator signal.

Bracket signal with movable slide route indicator.

Taken from the Railway Gazette

A heavy up train standing in Snow Hill.

Lens of Sutton

The scene in Snow Hill in 1913, looking north. Great Charles Street passed under the railway near the inner ends of the bay platforms, and passenger access from that street was given by a subway from which stairs led to both up and down sides near the brake van on the goods train at the far end of the station.

British Railways

The former Great Western Hotel in Colmore Row made a dignified frontage to the station. A Birmingham Corporation electric tramcar is waiting to leave Livery Street.
Lens of Sutton

and the lofty roof enabled smoke to rise and disperse without causing annoyance and discomfort to passengers. The whole was in marked contrast to the LNWR & MR station at New Street where the platforms were cramped and narrow, and the only access to some of them was from a narrow footbridge, itself a public right-of-way across the station. Indeed, the whole stood in marked contrast to the station at New Street as it is today, where the need to obtain a financial return commensurate with site value, has led to buildings being erected over the station, leaving conditions at platform level which many persons will find claustrophobic, and in which diesel fumes may linger for an uncomfortable length of time.

The rebuilding of the station at Snow Hill, together with the major changes in the track layout, meant that a completely new signalling system was needed. The company had been experimenting with power signalling at a number of smaller signal boxes such as Yarnton Junction, and the decision was taken to install such a system at Snow Hill. The Siemens Company built the electrical equipment, and the whole was operated from two signal boxes, that at the south end having 224 miniature levers, while the box at the north end had 80. Standard semaphore signals were used, but it was possible to keep their numbers to a minimum by the adoption of route indicators.

The rail approaches to the station were much improved, although little could be done over widening the tunnel. That apart, a scheme of quadrupling was put in hand, and was completed from Handsworth Junction to Olton, leaving the work from Olton to Lapworth to be dealt with after the First World War.

The main entrance to Snow Hill station for passengers was from Colmore Row where there was a long row of booking windows, all of which could be in use on busy summer Saturdays in later years. In this scene the large hanging sign directs passengers through an arch to the footbridge and so to platforms 7, 8, 9, 10, 11 and 12 for all stations to Leamington, Oxford, Reading, London, South of England, Stratford-on-Avon, Cheltenham, Gloucester, Bristol and West of England. The poster advertises day and half-day excursions by the shortest route to London for 8s. 6d. and 5s. 6d.
British Railways

Another view of the rebuilt Snow Hill station at its north end. The bay platforms on the left were little used for passenger traffic in later years.   *British Railways*

On a typical weekday in 1900, Snow Hill had some 70 passenger arrivals and departures at its north end, 50 at its south, while about 40 goods trains in each direction passed through the station. This simple statement does not fully demonstrate the traffic movements, however. While many of the passenger trains will have been through workings, others will have terminated or originated there, necessitating light engine or empty stock movements. There would have been numerous other shunting movements such as the detaching and attaching of slip coaches and vans for perishable traffic, and it should be remembered that this was still a time when passengers could have their horses and carriages conveyed by special vehicles on specified trains. The working at Snow Hill was certainly intensive, at least for most of the day.

The rebuilding and other improvements in and around central Birmingham had been largely completed by the end of 1912, the work having taken nearly seven years. The number of trains dealt with at Snow Hill certainly increased, although not dramatically so, but clearly they were handled with greater efficiency, and the works had been an essential prerequisite to the heavier trains which were to become part of the everyday scene. Snow Hill was a proud monument to Great Western achievement — it is sad to reflect that it was destined to have a working life of little more than 50 years.

No account of GWR developments in the Birmingham area would be complete without some mention of the efforts made by the company for the passenger from those parts who wished to travel to the continent. These might be said to have begun in 1897 when a portion for Folkestone Harbour began to be slipped at Reading from a morning express from Chester to Paddington. From Reading it was worked forward to Redhill and Tonbridge, there to be attached to the boat express at 2.45 p.m. from Charing Cross. In the reverse direction the boat express at 4.10 p.m. from Folkestone Harbour conveyed the portion for the GWR, which was slipped at Paddock Wood and

worked forward to Tonbridge, Redhill and Reading, where it was attached to a train from Paddington, going only as far as Shrewsbury and reached at about midnight. In the SER tables of Bradshaw, the service was described as 'Express Train to the Continent from Great Western Line', the converse in the opposite direction. By these services the Birmingham passenger could travel to or from Paris in a little under eleven hours.

In the summer of 1898, however, the style 'Continental Express' appeared in Bradshaw in the GWR tables against the times of a morning train from Chester, the working arrangements at Reading and over the SER being little changed from the previous year. In the reverse direction the portion for the GWR now connected with a later sailing, and did not leave Folkestone Harbour until 9.50 p.m. It was detached from the boat express to London during a stop at Tonbridge, and arrived in Reading in time to be attached to a newly-established train at 12.10 a.m. from Paddington, which Bradshaw also described as 'Continental Express'. The provision of a sleeping car on this train may well have been more with the continental passenger in mind than for those travelling from London. At this time there was no train in the reverse direction having the facility of a sleeping car.

The continental portion was withdrawn at the end of the summer of 1898, but it was restored for the summer of 1899. It is known that it then went through over the Mersey Railway to and from Liverpool Central (Low Level), and probably had done so in 1898. It was not revived in 1900, however, when, in any case, the Mersey Railway was involved with electrification. The summer of 1903 saw the introduction of a through service by day in each direction between Birkenhead and Dover; while not specifically described as a continental service, it terminated at Dover Harbour.

The continental passenger might well have been attracted by a further development in the autumn of 1905 when a late morning train from Birmingham commenced to slip a portion at Southall, to be worked forward via the West London line to Herne Hill, where it joined through coaches from both the LNWR and MR for Dover Harbour. Northbound the service was worked from Herne Hill (perhaps Victoria initially) via the West London line, this time to Paddington to be attached to an afternoon down express. The through services ceased at the end of the summer of 1908 but a working from Dover to Paddington only continued in the same times for several months afterwards.

The final stage of continental services began on 1st October 1910 with the introduction of a through train from Wolverhampton and Birmingham to Victoria station in London, and back. This was routed via Bicester, the Greenford loop, and the West London line, calling also at Kensington (Addison Road). Initially it enabled the traveller to reach Paris from Birmingham in 11¼ hours, rather less in the reverse direction leaving Paris at noon. This service was also described in Bradshaw as 'Continental Express'.

In connection with improved sailings on the cross-channel route via Flushing, there was a further development in May 1911. The train from Wolverhampton in a morning now included a SECR coach, going through to Queenborough Pier, returning to Wolverhampton by the evening train from Victoria. As the same time a through coach of the SECR was introduced in connection with the night sailings via Folkestone. This coach was worked south from Wolverhampton on a late-afternoon express, which stopped at Greenford for it to be detached, and it was then worked on to Victoria, calling at Ealing Broadway and Addison Road. In the northbound direction the coach arrived in Victoria on a boat train from Folkestone in the early morning, and it was taken via the West London line to Paddington to be attached to the 9.10 a.m. down express. In the July the Folkestone coach was extended to run to and from Shrewsbury.

The through coaches to and from Queenborough and Folkestone continued to operate into the autumn of 1911 but had ceased by February 1912. In that month the morning train from Wolverhampton to Victoria was still running, albeit without the return service in the evening, but it, too, was withdrawn soon afterwards, probably as an economy measure arising from the coal strike of that year.

Through GWR coach on the SECR at Herne Hill around 1905. The train also includes through vehicles from the LNWR and the Midland Railway.   *A. F. Selby, cty. John Minnis*

The station at Winchcombe under construction in September 1904.

British Railways

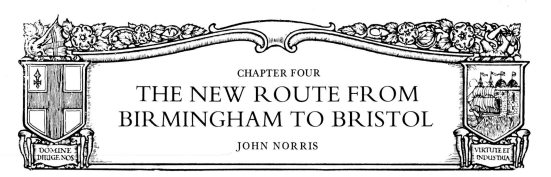

CHAPTER FOUR

THE NEW ROUTE FROM BIRMINGHAM TO BRISTOL

JOHN NORRIS

WHEN it came to developing a route of its own between Birmingham and Bristol, the GWR was able to exploit to the full a combination of existing facilities and the preparatory work done by others. The existing facilities included a line to Stratford from Honeybourne between Oxford and Worcester, originally a branch of the OWWR opened in 1859, while from Stratford to Hatton between Birmingham and Warwick, a line had been opened in 1860 as the Stratford-on-Avon Railway. These two short lines originally had separate terminal stations in Stratford but they had been connected in 1861, and a station for their joint use had been opened on the site of the present station in the Alcester Road on 1st January 1863. There was also the line between Cheltenham and Gloucester, most of which was owned jointly with the Midland company, while south from Gloucester the lines of the two companies ran side by side for much of the way to Standish. The GWR had running powers over the MR from Standish to Bristol, although it had not exercised them since 1886 when the Severn Tunnel was opened, and goods traffic could be sent that way between Bristol and Hereford, rather than incur tolls to the MR for the use of its line.

The gaps to be filled in making the existing lines part of a through route were, therefore, a new direct line from Birmingham to Stratford, another new line from Honeybourne to Cheltenham, and the restoration of a short length of line avoiding Gloucester, formerly part of the Cheltenham & Great Western Union Railway. Much of the planning for the first of these new lines had been undertaken by a company called the Birmingham, North Warwickshire & Stratford-upon-Avon Railway Company, incorporated in 1894. Its powers were to build a line from a separate terminus in Moor Street, Birmingham, to join the line from Broom Junction to Stratford, about a mile to the west of the Old Town station of the East & West Junction Railway (later to become part of the SMJR). Additionally it was to build a short connection to the GWR branch from Bearley to Alcester, the total new construction being 25 miles.

The Manchester, Sheffield & Lincolnshire Railway (later the GCR) was engaged with the construction of its extension to London which was to cross the East & West near Woodford, and it had obtained running powers to Stratford. The North Warwickshire Company was seen, therefore, as providing the Manchester company with access to Birmingham, the two companies being empowered by the Act of 1894 to enter into an agreement for the working and maintenance of the North Warwickshire by the Manchester. The East & West was

also given running powers to Birmingham by the intended new line.

As a means of making itself more attractive to investors, the North Warwickshire company obtained further powers in 1896 whereby it was to double at its own expense the line between its junction near Stratford and the junction near Woodford. The future GCR was deeply involved with its other developments, and did not pursue these opportunities to see its trains in Birmingham. It should also be

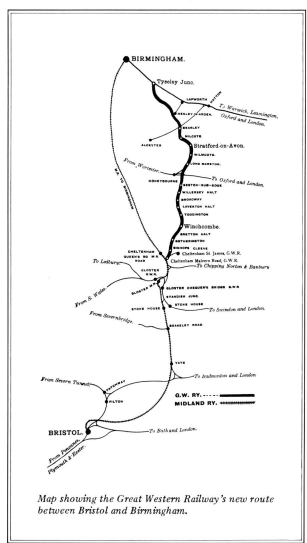

Map showing the Great Western Railway's new route between Bristol and Birmingham.

Two views of Wilmcote old station before a new station was built to the south of the bridge in association with the doubling of the line. *Top:* Looking north. *Bottom:* Looking south.

G. M. Perkins

remembered, however, that the GWR was actively assisting the GCR with their joint line through High Wycombe, so that the GWR may well have been in a position to indicate that an incursion of this nature would not be welcome. As it was, the North Warwickshire languished, and the GWR was able to step in, and under an Act of 1900 it secured the transfer to itself of the powers of that company, which had done nothing on the construction of its railway.

At Cheltenham the MSWJR was a contender for traffic, and it, too, had aspirations over access to Birmingham. In a burst of dynamism during the regime of Sam Fay as its general manager in the 1890s, it had come forward with a scheme for a line to Stratford from its own undertaking in the neighbourhood of Andoversford. Coupled with the scheme was a proposal that the MSWJR should work the North Warwickshire Railway when it was opened. Although it was some years before Fay took office at Marylebone, one may well wonder whether this example of his expansionist outlook influenced the GCR directors when they appointed him as their general manager. In the event, the scheme was defeated in the House of Lords in 1898, mainly because of doubts over the financial ability of the MSWJR to see it through, but coupled with a promise by the GWR to fill the gap northwards from Cheltenham by constructing the line to Honeybourne. Clearly it was to the advantage of the GWR to go ahead with such a line, and it obtained the necessary powers from parliament in 1899.

To meet the wishes of the GWR, the North Warwickshire company had formally abandoned its separate terminus in Birmingham in 1899, and had substituted a junction at Tyseley with the main line from Oxford to Birmingham. It had also abandoned the whole of its line southward to Stratford from the connection with the Alcester branch, and had withdrawn the running powers granted to the East & West. Subsequently the GWR revised the route of the North Warwickshire line to which it had succeeded, and introduced into the scheme a connection with the line from Hatton so that North Warwickshire trains could also use the station in Alcester Road, Stratford. The point of junction with the line from Hatton was at Bearley West, about ¾ mile from Bearley station.

The abandonment of the connection with the East & West was no loss to the GWR as another was available from a point near the Evesham Road crossing in Stratford, although probably little used. This connection had been brought into use soon after the opening of the East & West through to its station at Old Town, Stratford, on 1st July 1873.

The amount of new construction for the North Warwickshire Railway was thus reduced to about 18 miles. Just before reaching Bearley West, the Alcester branch had to be crossed, necessitating new connections and a new signal box to control them, known as Bearley North. Between Bearley North and Bearley station, about ½ mile,

Bearley North Junction signal box in about 1908 with 0—4—2T No. 523, the Alcester branch engine, standing alongside. The junction signal is for trains to Stratford-on-Avon to the right, and to Bearley station to the left.   *G. M. Perkins*

Excavating at Winchcombe. *British Railways*

Construction work in hand near Honeybourne West Junction in 1903. A down train on the Oxford-Worcester line is about to pass over the new bridge. The course of the new line from Cheltenham in the direction of Stratford passes under the bridge to the left, and the course of the west loop is in the foreground. *G. M. Perkins*

the branch was upgraded and made available for main-line trains, so that the North Warwickshire Railway became a useful diversionary route between Birmingham and Hatton.

South of Bearley station, the existing single line was doubled through to Honeybourne, with re-alignment and easing of the levels where this could be readily undertaken. The new line to Cheltenham left the old at Honeybourne East, about one mile short of Honeybourne station, and rejoined the GWR outside its terminal station at St. James, Cheltenham. At Honeybourne two short connections were made with the Oxford-Worcester line; one between the East and South Junctions gave through running to and from the directions of Stratford and Oxford (the East Loop), while the other between the West and North Junctions gave through running to and from the directions of Cheltenham and Worcester (the West Loop). The length of new construction was a little over 21 miles.

Between Honeybourne and Cheltenham, construction work started from the northern end during the winter of 1902/03. Sadly it had a disastrous start with the collapse in November 1903 of four arches in the partly-completed viaduct near Toddington, resulting in the death of four men and serious injury to seven others. An enquiry was conducted by the chief engineer of the LBSCR, and it

Arches at Toddington viaduct following the collapse in November 1903. *G. M. Perkins*

found that the cause of the collapse was the placing of a crane over the crown of one of the arches when there was insufficient timber support and the mortar was not sufficiently set. The viaduct became the main engineering feature of the new line, being 210 yards long and having 15 arches.

Toddington viaduct under construction, again showing the collapsed arches. *British Railways*

Huts for the accommodation of labourers at Toddington in 1904. The newly completed goods shed can be seen in the background.

British Railways

One purpose served by a station such as Toddington was the despatch of fruit, as is shown by the fruit baskets in the yard there, c.1905.

British Railways

Broadway station, looking north, shortly after opening.   *British Railways*

Towards the end of 1904 construction work was in hand at the Cheltenham end of the line. While the route had been planned to pass to the west of most of the built-up part of the town, some demolition of house property was inevitable, although clearly on nothing like the scale of that carried out in some densely populated towns half a century or so before. Nonetheless, it is arguable that the building of the Honeybourne line through Cheltenham represented the last occasion on which a town in this country was to see a main line of railway being driven through its midst. For people in Cheltenham displaced by the railway, the company built 42 houses in Alstone Avenue.

The opening of the line from Honeybourne to Cheltenham took place in short sections as construction work was completed, and passenger services commenced between Honeybourne and Broadway on Bank Holiday Monday, 1st August 1904, with an intermediate station at Weston-sub-Edge. On the following day an excursion was run for school parties from Broadway to Stratford, and this could well have been the first train to carry fare-paying passengers over the new direct line avoiding Honeybourne station. Although this section of line was not to have a regular passenger service over it until 1908, it had been

inspected and approved by the Board of Trade with the remainder of the line to Broadway.

It had been intended to operate a service of steam railmotors, both to Broadway and on some of the workings between Honeybourne and Stratford, but there were delays in building the new stock at Swindon, and nearly two months were to elapse before two cars arrived and commenced trial running. The full railmotor service commenced on 24th October 1904 and the first halts in the district, at Broad Marston, Chambers Crossing, and Evesham Road Crossing on the Stratford line, and at Willersey on the Broadway line, were brought into use on the same day.

Although arrangements were made for fruit to be carried over the new line from Toddington for despatch by rail from Broadway, formal opening of this section did not take place until 1st December 1904, and from Toddington to Winchcombe on 1st February 1905. Because of the work in constructing Greet tunnel (693 yards), the next section through to Bishop's Cleeve was not brought into use until 1st June 1906, and finally, on 1st August 1906, through working between Honeybourne and Cheltenham (St. James) became a reality. This entailed reversal at Malvern Road, but as all services at this time

GREAT WESTERN RAILWAY:

Opening of New Line
BETWEEN
BISHOP'S CLEEVE & CHELTENHAM.
TIME TABLE OF RAIL MOTOR SERVICE
(ONE CLASS ONLY)
CHELTENHAM, EVESHAM & STRATFORD-ON-AVON.
COMMENCING AUGUST 1st.—WEEK DAYS ONLY.

		a.m.		a.m.	a.m.	a.m.	p.m.	p.m.	p.m.	p.m.	p.m.	p.m.
London (Paddington) ...	dep.	...	...	5 40	...	9 0	10 50	11 45	1 40	1 10	3 15
Reading	"	...	...	6 41	...	9 51	11 42	12 30	2 0	2 0	3 28
Swindon	"	...	...	7 50	...	10 55	12 37	1 40	3 5	3 5	5 5
Hereford	"	...	...	7 45	...	9 55	—	2 5	—	4 10	6 25
Ledbury	"	...	...	8 30	...	10 30	—	1 58	—	4 27	—
Chipping Norton Jct. ...	"	...	...	8 58	...	—	1 0	—	3 20	4 50	—
Cardiff	"	...	...	7 55	...	10 23	...	12 48	1 25	1 25	6 8
Newport	"	...	...	8 20	...	10 48	...	1 10	1 55	1 55	6 30
Lydney	"	...	...	8 58	...	11 30	...	1 53	2 51	2 51	7 11
Gloucester	"	...	...	9 35	...	12 10	1 55	3 15	4 10	5 30	8 0

		a.m.		a.m.	a.m.		p.m.	p.m.	p.m.	p.m.	p.m.	p.m.
Cheltenham (St. James' Sq.)	dep.	8 5	...	10 1	...		12 38	2 35	3 38	5 10	5 8	8 40
Bishop's Cleeve	"	8 17	...	10 13	...		12 50	2 47	3 50	5 25	6 20	8 51
Gotherington	"	8 22	...	10 18	...		12 55	2 52	3 55	5 30	6 25	8 56
Gretton Halt	"	8 27	...	10 23	...		1 0	2 57	4 0	—	6 30	9 1
Winchcombe	"	8 32	...	10 28	...		1 5	3 2	4 5	5 39	6 35	9 6
Toddington	"	8 40	...	10 35	...		1 12	3 10	4 13	...	6 43	9 13
Laverton Halt	"	8 47	...	10 41	...		1 18	3 17	4 20	...	6 50	9 20
Broadway	"	8 55	...	10 49	11 35		1 26	3 24	4 27	...	6 57	9 26
Willersey Halt	"	8 59	...	10 53	11 39		1 30	3 28	4 31	...	7 1	9 30
Bretforton & Weston-sub-Edge	"	9 3	...	10 57	11 43		1 34	3 32	4 35	...	7 5	9 34
Honeybourne	arr.	9 10	...	11 3	11 50		1 40	3 40	4 42	...	7 12	9 40

							Via Evesham		Via Evesham			
Honeybourne	dep.	9M22	...	11 8	12 2			3 49		...	7 29	...
Moreton-in-Marsh ...	arr.	9M51	...	11 35	12 23		3 35	4 18	6 26	...	7 54	...
Oxford	"	10 45	...	12 41	1R7		4 15	5 33	7 7	...	9 10	...
London (Paddington) ...	"	12 15	...	2 15	2R33		5 50	7 15	8V50	...	10 50	...
Honeybourne	dep.	9 19	...	11M12			1 46		4M46	...	7M45	...
Stratford-on-Avon {	arr.	9 41	...	11M34			2 9		5M14	...	8M12	...
{	dep.	9 45	...				2 30		5 20	...	...	...
Leamington	arr.	10 23	...	12 46			3 3		6 2	...	9 7	...
Birmingham (Snow Hill)	"	10 34	...	12M30			3 47		6 45	...	9 40	...
London (Paddington) ...	"	1 53	...	3 25			5 20		8V50	...	...	...
Honeybourne	dep.	9 29	...	...	11M51		1M42	3M42	5 21	...	7 19	9M41
Littleton and Badsey ...	arr.	9 35	...	...	12 3		1M49	3M49	5 27	...	8 6	...
Evesham	"	9 41	...	...	12M1		1M55	3M55	5 37	...	7 27	9M58
Worcester (Shrub Hill) ...	"	10 18	...	...	12 40			4 41	6 12	...	7 50	10 39

		a.m.		a.m.		a.m.	a.m.	p.m.	p.m.	p.m.	p.m.	p.m.
Worcester (Shrub Hill)	dep.	6 32		9 12		10 20	11 25	1 0	3 0	...	4 50	6 40
Evesham	"	7M32		9M45		10 53	12M35	2M0	4M25	...	5 23	7 18
Littleton and Badsey ...	"	7M52		9M52		10 58	12M42	2M7	4M32	...	5 28	7 21
Honeybourne	arr.	7M45		9M58		11 8	12M48	2M13	4M38	...	5 33	7 26
London (Paddington) ...	dep.	...	—					6 30		...	2 15	—
Birmingham (Snow Hill)	"	...	—	7 30		9B45	10 20	12 35		...	4 5	5B55
Leamington	"	...	—	7 40		—	10 42	12 40		...	4 20	5 25
Stratford-on-Avon {	arr.	...	—	8M25		10B28	11 25	1 27		...	5 8	—
{	dep.	...	—	8M30		10M33	11 35	1M35		...	5M35	6 40
Honeybourne	arr.	...	—	8M54		10M58	11 54	2M 4		...	6M 4	6 58
London (Paddington) ...	dep.	...	...	5 40		...	9 45	10 20	1 45	...	...	4X55
Oxford	"	...	...	7 58		...	11 22	12 8	3 8	...	3 42	6X20
Moreton-in-Marsh ...	"	...	...	9M55		...	12 7	1 4	3 51	...	4 57	7 3
Honeybourne	arr.	...	...	10M23		...	Via Evshm.	1 25	Via Evshm.	...	5 18	7 19
Honeybourne	dep.	7 46		10 26		11 15	12 49	2 14	4 39	...	6 12	7 34
Bretforton & Weston-sub-Edge	"	7 53		10 33		11 22	12 56	2 21	4 46	...	6 19	7 40
Willersey Halt	"	7 57		10 37		11 26	1 0	2 25	4 50	...	6 23	7 44
Broadway	"	8 4		10 44		11 32	1 6	2 32	4 56	...	6 29	7 50
Laverton Halt	"	8 10		10 50		...	1 12	2 40	5 2	...	6 35	7 56
Toddington	"	8 17		10 57		...	1 19	2 45	5 9	...	6 42	8 2
Winchcombe	"	8 24		11 4		...	1 27	2 55	5 18	5 45	6 51	8 10
Gretton Halt	"	8 30		11 10		...	1 33	3 1	5 24	...	6 57	8 15
Gotherington	"	8 35		11 16		...	1 38	3 6	5 29	5 52	7 2	8 20
Bishop's Cleeve	"	8 39		11 21		...	1 42	3 10	5 33	5 58	7 6	8 24
Cheltenham (St. James' Sq.)	arr.	8 51		11 34		...	1 54	3 22	5 45	6 11	7 18	8 35
Gloucester	arr.	9 9		12 10		...	2 25	4 12	6 5	6 35	7 50	10 2
Lydney	"	10 0		12 48		...	4 8	5 45	6 54	8 10	9 32	1 16
Newport	"	10 59		1 26		...	5 12	5 52	8 5	9 7	10 16	1 58
Cardiff	"	11 21		1 50		...	5 42	6 14	8 35	9 35	10 40	2 21
Chipping Norton Jct. ...	"	...		12 27		...	4 20	...	8 5	...	8 5	...
Ledbury	"	11 21		1 17		...	4 15	—	7 40	7 40	—	...
Hereford	"	10 56		1 54		...	4 52	—	7 20	—	10 15	...
Swindon	"	10 42		...		...	3 46	6 48	8 19	8 19	9 22	1 35
Reading	"	11 41		...		...	4 42	8 19	9 20	9 20	10 38	2 40
London (Paddington) ...	"	12 20		...		...	5 33	8D30	10 10	10 10	11 45	3Y30

B Monday, August 6th, excepted. D Dining Car Swindon to London. M Rail Motor Car, one class only. R Luncheon Car between Oxford and London. V Dining Car between Leamington, Oxford and London. X Sleeping Car Gloucester to Paddington. Y Dining Car between Paddington and Oxford. † Birmingham arrive 1.25 p.m. on August 6th.

TICKETS.—Passengers desiring to travel by the Motor Cars from the Stations must get their tickets at the Station Booking Offices, and must produce them on entering the Cars. Passengers joining the Cars at the "Halts" will receive their tickets from Conductor on the Car.

PARCELS.—Parcels will be conveyed between the Stations only, and not from the "Halts."

SMOKING.—Passengers are respectfully requested to refrain from Smoking and Spitting in the Motor Cars.

PUNCTUALITY.—The Company have the greatest desire to make the Motor Car Service punctual and the public can very materially assist in that direction if they would be alert in getting in and out of the Cars.

THE ROAD MOTOR SERVICE between Cheltenham and Bishop's Cleeve will be discontinued after July 31st.

PADDINGTON, July, 1906.

JAMES C. INGLIS, General Manager.

(31,500) G.D. 176. WYMAN & SONS, Ltd., Printers, Fetter Lane, London, E.C., and Reading.—5402a.

Bishops Cleeve station. *Top:* Looking north. *Bottom:* Looking south.   *Lens of Sutton*

A view of Winchcombe station with southbound railmotor at the platform.   *Lens of Sutton*

were worked by railmotors, it did not create a serious operating problem. A station at Malvern Road was opened on 30th March 1908, having a single island platform with a short bay at the north end for the use of the Honeybourne services.

A service of road motor buses from the railway company's own fleet was instituted between Winchcombe and Cheltenham simultaneously with the opening of the railway to Winchcombe, and was available to passengers who had made through bookings via the new line to and from Cheltenham and beyond. The *Cheltenham Chronicle* reported that the pioneer vehicle on the service was a Milnes-Daimler of 20-24 h.p., with seats for twenty passengers, and that it carried a Cornwall registration, AF 74, having been displaced from the service between Helston and the Lizard, which had been withdrawn as the result of a dispute between the company and the local authority as to rolling the roads. Only three trips were made each day, taking 1½ hours between the two railway stations, compared with 25-30 minutes when the railmotors commenced running. When the railway was extended from Winchcombe to Bishop's Cleeve, the motor bus service was revised accordingly.

Between Honeybourne and Bearley station, most of the doubling was completed and brought into use during the first half of 1907, and much of the remainder in December of that year. In August 1907 part of the new bridge being built across the River Avon south of Stratford fell, blocking the existing single line, and this event

may well have been a cause of delay to the works. It may be noted that the line between Hatton and Bearley was allowed to remain single, not being doubled until 1939.

In contrast to the line from Honeybourne to Cheltenham, no attempt was made to open the North Warwickshire Railway in short sections. At no point was it more than about five miles from the main line from Birmingham to Oxford, and for much of its distance it passed through a rural countryside with few villages. The only place of consequence which it was to serve was Henley-in-Arden, and that was already served by a branch from Rowington Junction on the Oxford line. Although possible housing development nearer Birmingham around Hall Green, Yardley Wood and Shirley, offered longer-term possibilities for local traffic, the immediate interest of the GWR was its use as a through route.

Construction started in September 1905 and the works were sufficiently far advanced for a party of directors and senior officials of the company to be conveyed in a contractor's train throughout from Bearley to Tyseley in November 1906. There were few engineering difficulties, a tunnel at Wood End being the only feature calling for mention, and the approach cutting and the bore of 175 yards were all completed within the space of eleven months during 1906. Most other excavations and brickwork were completed in 1906 and the line opened for goods traffic on 9th December 1907, for passengers on 1st July 1908.

Site for station at Henley-in-Arden on the North Warwickshire line being excavated in 1906, looking north. *G. M. Perkins*

More construction work at Henley-in-Arden. Seen here are the abutments of a bridge being built to carry the connection between the new station and the terminus of the branch from Rowington Junction over the Birmingham road. *G. M. Perkins*

A steam navvy at work in the cutting at Crocketts Farm, north of Henley-in-Arden, in 1906.   *G. M. Perkins*

Tipping in progress north of Henley-in-Arden.   *G. M. Perkins*

Contractors for the North Warwickshire line had a temporary locomotive shed near the site of the station for Henley-in-Arden. In this view two Manning Wardle 0–6–0Ts, *Sidley* and *Newport*, are seen outside the shed. *G. M. Perkins*

A contractor's train with a Manning Wardle locomotive on the works near Henley-in-Arden. *G. M. Perkins*

New overbridge spanning the road from Ullenhall to Henley-in-Arden in 1906, looking towards Henley.   *G. M. Perkins*

Station at Danzey, c.1908.   *Collection R. S. Carpenter*

The initial local passenger service was provided by steam railmotors, a few of which ran to Bearley to make connections, rather than to Stratford. At the northern end of the line few of the services ran through to Birmingham, passengers being required to change at Tyseley. With the introduction of the railmotors, the old branch to Henley-in-Arden was extended to the North Warwickshire station for the town, so that passengers had a choice of route to Birmingham. The old branch terminus was closed to passengers, however, but continued in use as a goods station.

Simultaneously with the start of the railmotor service, the long-awaited introduction took place of a new express between Wolverhampton and Penzance, calling only at Stratford and Cheltenham (Malvern Road) between Birmingham and Bristol, for which the short avoiding line at Gloucester had been relaid, and the connection at Standish had been restored. But a snag had arisen in that the MR had challenged the way in which the GWR proposed to operate its new trains over the Midland line.

Originally the Bristol & Gloucester Railway had been broad gauge, using the Cheltenham & Great Western Union line to gain access to Gloucester from Standish. The GWR had running powers over the Bristol & Gloucester. The latter company had, however, passed into the control of the MR, which converted the Bristol line to mixed gauge south of Standish, and built a line of its own on the standard gauge from there into Gloucester, the broad gauge rails being left in deference to the running powers of the GWR. In 1863 the GWR entered into a far-reaching agreement with the MR, granting the MR running powers from Worcester to Hereford and into South Wales. This agreement was primarily to pre-empt opposition by the MR to the amalgamation of the West Midland Railway with the GWR, but it also contained a clause whereby the MR extended the running powers of the GWR to the standard gauge on the former Bristol & Gloucester line.

The GWR used the running powers over the standard gauge line to work goods traffic between Bristol and Hereford via Gloucester but they had been dormant since the diversion of that traffic to the route through the Severn Tunnel in 1886. The question of their use had arisen again in 1895 when the GWR proposed to build a line from its intended South Wales & Bristol Direct Railway at Old Sodbury, to the Severn & Wye Railway between Berkeley Road and Sharpness; the Severn & Wye had passed into the joint ownership of the GWR and MR in the previous year. The GWR line from Old Sodbury would have been about 14 miles in length, and would have passed about two miles to the east of the MR line from Bristol before turning to the west to cross it some way south of Berkeley Road station. The two companies then agreed that the GWR should construct connections with the MR where the South Wales & Bristol Direct crossed it near Yate; the GWR would also make its connection with the Severn & Wye but from a junction with the MR south of Berkeley Road. The connection at Standish would also be restored.

It was over the connections at Standish and Yate that the GWR intended to run its new express trains from Wolverhampton and Birmingham to Bristol and the West Country. The MR now claimed, however, that the purpose of the connections at Yate was for the GWR to work traffic to and from the Severn & Wye line, and nothing else. Accordingly the GWR took the matter to the courts, seeking a declaration that it was entitled to use the connections at Yate for any of the traffic which it worked over the Bristol & Gloucester line. The MR was hardly in a position to challenge the right of the GWR to run on and off its line at Standish, but it did see this opportunity to exact the maximum toll from GWR trains running between Birmingham and Bristol by ensuring that they went over the additional ten miles of Midland line between Yate and Bristol.

The case was heard by Mr. Justice Warrington towards the end of May 1908, and he gave judgment in favour of the MR. From the evidence given it is apparent that the MR had refused to co-operate over the completion of the junction at Yate, one of its engineers telling the court that two months before there were gaps of 110 feet and 242 yards respectively between the completed portions of the GWR connecting lines at Yate and the actual junctions. As a result, when the new GWR service began on 1st July 1908, it ran over the MR from Yate into Bristol via Fishponds.

The matter went to the Court of Appeal in the October when the Master of the Rolls gave judgment in favour of the GWR, saying that the running powers over the connections at Yate were not confined to Severn & Wye traffic, but were perfectly general. Lord Justice Moulton and Lord Justice Farrell agreed, the latter pointing out the question of convenience to the public which was ignored by the MR but was mentioned in the relevant Act. And so on 2nd November 1908 the new express service commenced running by its intended route.

Both the North Warwickshire Railway and the line from Honeybourne to Cheltenham had been skilfully engineered with easy curves and an absence of severe gradients. Indeed, heavy goods trains from South Wales to the industrial heartland of the country could run the whole way from Newport to Stratford without encountering a gradient more serious than that at 1 in 108 for about half-a-mile on leaving Cheltenham. The start from Stratford then entailed a pull at 1 in 75 for about 1¼ miles away from the valley of the Avon; however, this was a part of the original line of 1860 and the gradient had been reduced in length during the widening and other improvements carried out in 1907. Then soon after leaving Bearley there began a rise of ten miles to Earlswood, mostly at 1 in 150. Although all the new works had been planned so as to avoid the use of assistant engines, some trains certainly did obtain assistance at Stratford, perhaps just as far as Wilmcote but otherwise through to Earlswood.

The new route was certainly much easier to work than that via Hereford and Worcester, and upon the opening of the North Warwickshire Railway several trains were immediately diverted to run via Cheltenham and Stratford. These included a small number of trains which had used the single line from Gloucester to Ledbury on their way to Worcester and beyond, such being the problems of getting all the traffic through. The line from Gloucester

Bristol-Birmingham express approaching Henley-in-Arden c.1910 with an 'Atbara' class locomotive.   *G. M. Perkins*

to Ledbury had been kept open all night to pass these trains but this became unnecessary, thus achieving one small economy.

While passenger trains also benefited from the easy gradients, they were also free from speed restrictions arising from sharp curvature; between Honeybourne and Cheltenham there were no curves having a radius of less than 40 chains, other than at junctions. As a route for fast passenger trains between Birmingham and South Wales, development did not come until after the First World War. The through trains to and from the West Country quickly became established, and it was mainly with these trains that the new lines scored their greatest passenger success. They were indeed invaluable with the growth in holiday travel during the 1930s when the GWR was able to offer a service of trains starting from Wolverhampton and Birmingham, whereas by the rival route trains would normally have come from much further afield and so be heavily loaded by the time they reached Birmingham.

Soon after the line was completed from Honeybourne, the Cheltenham newspapers were carrying reports of special trains and diversions, some of which undoubtedly ran to or from Birmingham via Stratford and Hatton in 1907. In the November of that year there occurred a fall of rock in Colwall tunnel between Worcester and Hereford, and the situation was relieved to a great extent by the ease with which diversions could be made via Honeybourne.

Also in 1907 the GWR was concerned about the competition for passenger traffic to Stratford from London. It was hardly in a favourable position because its

distance of 121 miles via Oxford and Leamington compared with only 93 miles from Marylebone via Woodford by the GCR and SMJR. The best that the GWR could offer was 2 hrs 35 mins by two trains daily, whereas the GCR/SMJR could offer three services in 2 hrs 15 mins, 2 hrs 20 mins and 2 hrs 35 mins respectively. Even the LNWR and SMJR between them could improve on the best GWR times by five minutes once a day via Blisworth from Euston. The response of the GWR was to institute a slip portion at Moreton-in-Marsh off the 4.45 p.m. down express, then non-stop from Paddington to Worcester. This commenced in July 1907 and gave an arrival at Stratford in 2 hrs 20 mins for the 110 miles.

The slip at Moreton is of further interest, however, in that it comprised two coaches which were worked forward from Moreton over the east loop at Honeybourne to the East Junction signal box where they were separated, the front coach being for Stratford and the rear for Cheltenham (St. James). The time to Cheltenham by this service was 2 hrs 50 mins, an improvement of ten minutes or so over the best times from Paddington via Swindon and Gloucester. No attempt was made to give Stratford an improved working in the opposite direction, the slip coach being worked to Worcester later the same evening, and returned to Paddington by a morning train next day. The Cheltenham coach was, however, used to provide a working in the opposite direction, running by the same route to Moreton, there to be attached to the 5.35 p.m. from Worcester to Paddington.

The arrangements for the slip at Moreton were unchanged in November 1914. The Stratford coach appears to have been withdrawn soon afterwards, however, but a coach for Cheltenham continued to be slipped until the end of 1916. While it was in operation, the Stratford coach had given rise to what were probably the only regular passenger services over the east loop at Honeybourne, the surviving Cheltenham coach being worked in and out of Honeybourne station in each direction. Except for breaks in wartime, a train continued to run from Cheltenham to Moreton to connect with equivalent trains right up to the cessation of local services between Cheltenham and Honeybourne in 1960, and this likewise reversed in Honeybourne station.

Another development affecting Cheltenham was the opening of a station for the racecourse in 1912; this was between Malvern Road and Bishop's Cleeve. It was open only on race days but clearly it will have generated much useful revenue for the railway, which operated race specials or cheap bookings from many parts of the system for all the principal meetings. The railway also passed near the racecourse at Stratford, and a station was opened there, although not until 1933.

Even before the North Warwickshire line was opened to passengers, the GWR had realised that the growth in local traffic was likely to be such that it would be difficult to handle it all at Snow Hill. Accordingly the idea of a separate terminal station at Moor Street was revived. Parliamentary powers were obtained in June 1908, and building work was pushed ahead rapidly, being sufficiently far advanced for passenger traffic to begin on 1st July 1909. Moor Street was long regarded as being the station for the North Warwickshire line, while local trains for Solihull and the Leamington line used Snow Hill. There was good reason for the arrangement as it reduced the number of conflicting movements over the junctions at Tyseley.

Moor Street station became known for the use of traversers for releasing engines arriving with trains at its terminal platforms. The traversers were a form of platform with rails on to which an engine would run; it would then be moved laterally until the rails were in line with an adjoining track, along which the engine could be released. They were large enough to accommodate the largest 4–6–0 classes with tender.

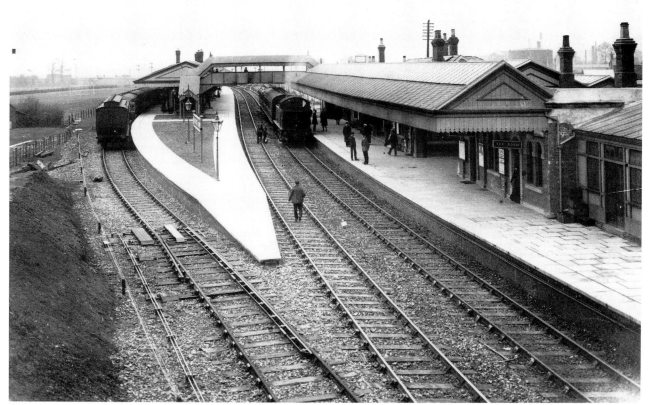

Stratford-on-Avon station, looking north from the Alcester Road.   *British Railways*

Although not necessarily realised at the time, these two locomotives awaiting departure at Paddington around 1909 are symbolic of the thorough modernisation carried out within the short time of ten years. Dean 7 ft 8 in single-wheeler No. 3049 *Nelson* represents the final modification to the class, the boiler having a raised Belpaire firebox and drum-type smokebox. Across the platform is a Churchward 2-cylinder 4–6–0 of the 'Saint' class representing the new order and presenting an outline which remained familiar until the end of steam.

Collection J. E. Kite

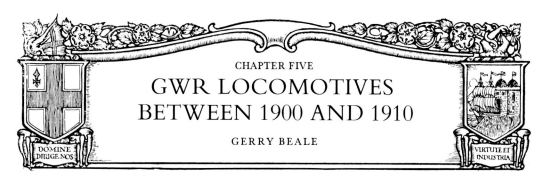

CHAPTER FIVE

GWR LOCOMOTIVES
BETWEEN 1900 AND 1910

GERRY BEALE

THE first decade of the present century was a time of enormous change on the Great Western Railway. Emerging at last from the doldrums of the 1890s and led by a dynamic and innovative management, within this relatively short space of time the line emerged as one of the leading railway companies of the Edwardian age. The purpose of this review of GWR locomotive matters during this outstanding era is to focus on the striding achievements of these few years, to present an analysis of events, and illustrate just how dramatic was the change. The majority of these notes are based on the late H. Holcroft's classis work *An Outline of Great Western Locomotive Practice*, and this book, currently out of print, is recommended to anyone who wishes to have a more detailed, if rather biased, account of this fascinating subject. Holcroft himself was an ardent admirer of G. J. Churchward, being employed in the drawing office at Swindon during this exciting period, and having more than a little involvement in the development work.

Churchward was elevated to the position of Locomotive Carriage and Wagon Superintendent early in the decade and quickly set about introducing his new classes. But prior to 1910 their numbers were few compared with the ranks of Dean and Armstrong locomotives, and to fully appreciate the events of the first ten years of the present century, and their significance, it is necessary to take a look back over the last years of the nineteenth.

When Brunel's broad gauge finally passed away in 1892 no doubt the Board of Directors were glad to see it go, but many sentimentalists mourned its passing and felt the GWR could never be the same again. No sooner had the work of conversion in Devon and Cornwall been completed than the company embarked on a vast programme of upgrading work which would permit the use of heavier locomotives than had been the case on the broad gauge. So far as the west of England was concerned, much of the route mileage required doubling, a task not completed until 1930, Brunel's timber viaducts needed replacing, on many other bridges strengthening was necessary, and the majority of track needed renewal with bullhead rails and transverse sleepers. Similar work was required on lines throughout the system and inevitably this engineering work took its toll on train working. It was not only the indirect route to the west which earned the GWR the title of the 'Great Way Round'!

During this period of renewal, trains were entirely in the hands of locomotives of Armstrong and Dean design. Much of the express work to the West of England was handled by William Dean's 7 ft 8 in single-wheelers of

the 'Achilles' class, considered by many to be the most elegant and beautifully proportioned locomotives ever built. Certainly they marked a high point in locomotive design during the late Victorian era, at least so far as the GWR was concerned, a fact which is all the more remarkable when one considers the earlier appearance of

G. J. CHURCHWARD

the class when running as broad gauge 2—2—2 'convertibles'.

The single-wheelers worked express passenger trains between Paddington and Newton Abbot with occasional trips to South Wales. West of Newton Abbot, trains were handled by ex-broad gauge 0—4—4 tanks of the '3521' class which had been reduced in gauge. The singles rarely strayed from this route and it was not until the turn of the century that they appeared elsewhere. Construction continued until 1899 and, although single-wheelers generally became obsolescent early in the 20th century, they put in much useful work.

In 1894 there appeared from Swindon a small class of four-coupled engines of similar outline to the 'singles'. Although on record as being reconstructed from some earlier experimental locomotives, of both broad and narrow gauges, probably only the wheel centres were re-used, the boilers, cylinders and valve gear being new and identical to the 'Achilles' class, thus allowing some

Dean 'Single' No. 3014 *Iron Duke* was built in 1892 and is seen here at Old Oak Common in the livery applied from 1906. She was one of the earliest of the class to be withdrawn from service in 1908, but all had gone by the end of 1915.   *Collection R. C. Riley*

interesting comparisons to be made. Apparently, the 'Armstrongs', as the class became known, did not distinguish themselves and they regularly worked on semifast passenger, fast goods and perishable trains on the London-Bristol main line. However, they were of importance in that they were the first double-framed 4—4—0s on the GWR and they set the pattern for subsequent 4—4—0 classes for a considerable period.

Passenger trains on other routes of the GWR were worked by the numerous classes of 2—2—2 and 2—4—0 tender locomotives produced by both William Dean and his predecessor Joseph Armstrong. The single-wheelers of the 'Sir Daniel', 'Sir Alexander' and 'Cobham' classes, and the 2—4—0s of such types as the 'Chancellors', 'Stellas' and 'Barnums', had their origins back in the earliest days of the narrow gauge on the GWR. They had

No. 16 *Brunel* was the first of the 'Armstrongs' to be rebuilt with a Belpaire boiler in 1901. In later years all four members of the class received standard No. 2 coned boilers and were eventually assimilated into the 'Flower' class.   *L & GRP, cty. David & Charles*

been produced and continuously updated at both Swindon and Wolverhampton works.

Indeed, until 1896, Wolverhampton enjoyed a large measure of independence from Swindon, and Northern Division locomotives, built and repaired at Stafford Road works, were instantly recognisable from their Swindon counterparts. George Armstrong's retirement, after 30 years in charge of the Northern Division, precipitated the gradual dominance of Swindon over Wolverhampton and

Oxford, early in the twentieth century the majority of the 'Rivers' were moved to the Bristol division where they worked trains to Paddington and the west of England. A number were always to be found at Trowbridge where their duties included trains to Salisbury and Weymouth as well as other local services.

Main line stopping, suburban and branch working was handled by an army of tank engines of 2-4-0, 0-4-2 and 0-6-0 types. The four-coupled tanks could be found

Dean's attractive 'River' class 2-4-0s were to be found principally in the Bristol Division. Here No. 72 *Wye* leaves Dunball station on a typical passenger working.

L & GRP, cty. David & Charles

by the time of Churchward's appointment in 1902 this move was practically complete.

Around the time of the abolition of the broad gauge, it had been proposed that Stafford Road should become the principal locomotive works of the GWR. Swindon would have had responsibility for carriage and wagon construction and repair, with repairs only to locomotives working in the south and west of England. However, sufficient land could not be acquired at Wolverhampton for the necessary expansion of the works and consequently Swindon retained its dominance in GWR locomotive matters.

It was during this period that the last new class of 2-4-0 tender engine entered traffic. The 'River' class emerged from Swindon between 1895 and 1897 and were in fact renewals of earlier single-wheelers. This elegant class was the last to be constructed with sandwich frames, consisting of thin sheets of steel separated by thick hardwood blocks, a feature which had its origins in Gooch's first narrow gauge design of 1855. Initially allocated to

everywhere, in both Swindon and Wolverhampton guises, working anything from heavy suburban trains from Paddington along the Thames Valley, to small mixed branch trains on West Country branch lines. As a general rule, however, the London division preferred 2-4-0 tanks of the 'Metro' class for its suburban services, whereas the Birmingham and Wolverhampton areas favoured 0-4-2 tanks for these duties. The 0-6-0s, almost without exception carrying saddle tanks and appearing in many forms depending on where they were maintained, often worked on the same duties, and in addition were used for the majority of the shunting work. Those with 4 ft 7½ in diameter driving wheels, both inside and double-framed, worked many heavy goods and mineral trains on the main lines in addition to the 'Standard Goods' tender classes of both Dean and Armstrong. William Dean's famous '2301' class first appeared in 1883 and construction continued until 1898 when the type numbered 260. A surprisingly large amount of main line goods work was handled by tank locomotives and

A small detachment of the 'army of tank engines' at Old Oak Common. This particular group's duties consisted, for the most part, of empty carriage 'pilot' working in and out of Paddington.   *A. C. Roberts*

many water stops were necessary. Conversely, many of the goods tender engines worked on passenger trains including fast turns.

In 1895 several events occurred which were to have far-reaching effects for the Great Western, both on train working and in locomotive design. Firstly, the compulsory stop at Swindon Junction was abolished. Since 1841 the refreshment rooms had been run by contractors and, as part of the agreement, all regular trains had to call in order to allow passengers to partake of the facilities. Eventually, the GWR bought out the contractors for the astonishing figure, for the time, of £100,000 and from 1st October two trains daily, in each direction, passed Swindon at speed. From 1897 Dean's single-wheelers were able to run non-stop from London to Exeter via the Bristol goods avoiding lines and to Newport via the Severn Tunnel, due in no small part to the provision of water troughs at Goring in the Thames Valley and Foxes Wood near Bristol.

The second and even more important event of 1895 was the appointment of George Jackson Churchward as Assistant Locomotive Works Manager. Churchward had previously been Manager of the Carriage Works where, amongst othe innovations, the first corridor train to run in Britain had been introduced, and it is worth taking a look at this great man's career thus far.

When the Great Western absorbed the South Devon Railway in 1876, quite apart from the obvious territorial

gains, additional route mileage etc., they acquired two important assets which were probably unrealised at the time, namely James C. Inglis, whose contribution to the expansion of the GWR has already been examined, and G. J. Churchward.

A Devonian by birth, Churchward spent his childhood years at Stoke Gabriel on the banks of the River Dart. In 1873, at the age of sixteen, he became an articled pupil of John Wright, Locomotive Carriage and Wagon Superintendent of the SDR, at the company's works at Newton Abbot. Shortly after the amalgamation Churchward moved to Swindon to complete the last year of his pupillage under Joseph Armstrong where the prospects were considerably brighter for able young engineers.

Following Armstrong's sudden death in 1877, William Dean was appointed to the position of Locomotive, Carriage and Wagon Superintendent and Churchward had a new chief. From this time onwards he was concerned mostly with carriage and wagon development, a situation which was probably highly frustrating to an enthusiastic locomotive engineer, but he also worked in other departments. Some time was spent in the drawing office and between 1880 and 1882 he assisted Armstrong's son, 'Young Joe', with the design work for the GWR's outstandingly successful vacuum brake.

Throughout this period, and indeed throughout his career, Churchward took an interest in railway engineering progress not only in Great Britain but also in Europe and

A scene typical of the early years of the century at Worcester Shrub Hill. An Armstrong 'Standard Goods' No. 22 arrives from the Hereford direction as a '517' 0–4–2T shunts vans in the down bay platform.   *Collection J. E. Kite*

No. 2753 of the '2721' class was built in 1900. This view, taken at a yard in the Newport area, shows the crew, shunters and other railway staff proudly standing in front of 'their' engine.   *Collection Ian Cripps*

An unidentified 'Duke' class leaving Penzance with an up train. This view highlights the work necessary to upgrade the main line in the West of England by replacing the wooden viaducts and adding a second running line. The viaduct shown here was not replaced until 1921 when a stone embankment was substituted.

Collection J. E. Kite

the USA. It was this wide outlook and an ability to adopt the best principles of his contemporaries and apply them to his own work, that set Churchward apart from other engineers. From this background came the seeds which, when sown, evolved into the startling new designs of the early years of the twentieth century.

By 1895 William Dean had reached the peak of his career and the question of his successor was having to be faced. Dean's reputation was based on the glorious 7 ft 8 in single-wheelers and the outstanding '2301' standard goods engines but there were a number of new classes which were still to appear under his aegis. In the same year that Churchward transferred to the locomotive works, a new class of 4—4—0 tender engines was under construction. Known as the 'Duke of Cornwall' class, these locomotives, with their light 15 ton axle loading, were intended to work trains west of Newton Abbot over the ex-broad gauge lines. This route had only just been brought up to a standard sufficient to allow the use of larger locomotives but, even so, a particularly small tender had to be provided to allow the engines to be

turned on the small turntables in use in the far west. The new engines had bogies, frames and valve arrangements which closely followed the 4—2—2s while the boiler was based on the '2301' type, but with a longer barrel. One new feature was the extended smokebox which incorporated an American pattern of spark arrester. In this it is possible to discern evidence of Churchward already making his presence felt by applying a practice from abroad, so soon after his arrival in the locomotive works.

Although the GWR was provided with a plentiful supply of 0—6—0s, of both tank and tender variety, which were adequate for the majority of goods work, they were rapidly becoming outdated and underpowered for the increasingly heavy coal traffic which flowed from South Wales to Swindon and London. In 1896, therefore, a new 4—6—0 appeared incorporating inside cylinders, double frames and 4 ft 7½ inch diameter coupled wheels. Having a boiler with a raised round-top firebox and an extended smokebox, this first Great Western 4—6—0 looked very much like an extended 'Duke of Cornwall'

The 'Dukes' (sometimes known as the 'Pendennis Castle' class) were built principally for work over the hills of Devon and Cornwall. No. 3270 *Trevithick* is seen here, in original condition, squeezed onto the turntable at Penzance.   *Collection R. S. Carpenter*

'Badminton' class 4—4—0 No. 3302 *Charles Mortimer* passing Saltford on an up express, the first two vehicles of which are Travelling Post Office vans.   *L & GRP, cty. David & Charles*

'Badminton' class 4−4−0 No. 3297 *Earl Cawdor* in original condition. In 1903 it received an extremely large boiler with round-topped firebox and a side window cab which transformed its appearance. *Collection Gerry Beale*

type. Numbered 36, she was known universally as 'the Crocodile' and for some years worked coal trains from South Wales, through the Severn Tunnel to Swindon. On these duties she could do the work of two 0−6−0s but No. 36 was evidently deemed unsuccessful for she was destined to remain the only one of her type. When her boiler became due for renewal in 1905, instead of a replacement being provided, the locomotive was scrapped.

In 1896 Churchward was appointed Locomotive Works Manager and this placed him directly in line to succeed William Dean. Indeed, Dean's mental powers were

beginning to fail him and the hand of Churchward became ever more apparent in all subsequent designs to appear from Swindon. In 1897 he received further promotion to the position of Chief Assistant Locomotive Superintendent, in addition to retaining his former post.

During the same year the first of a new class of 4−4−0s with 6 ft 8½ in coupled wheels appeared. Intended for use between London and Bristol as replacements for the 'singles' which, with their limited adhesion, were becoming a little outclassed on the heaviest trains, they were known as the 'Badmintons'. Churchward's influence was discern-

Dean's double-framed 4−6−0 No. 36 'The Crocodile' never strayed far from Swindon and went for scrap in 1905. *Collection John Lewis*

An assembly of Armstrong, Dean and Churchward engines at Exeter shed early in the century.

British Railways

Although built as a 'Duke', No. 3312 carried the first standard No. 2 boiler, albeit with a dome. It thus became the prototype for the famed 'Bulldog' class and is shown here, on 15th October 1904, in original condition. *Collection J. E. Kite*

ible in the boiler which incorporated a Belpaire firebox, the first class on the GWR to carry this distinctive feature. Boilers on other members of the class included a number of experimental features, most of which were short-lived, but otherwise the locomotives followed the pattern of the 'Armstrong' class with inside cylinders and double frames.

With the arrival of the 'Badmintons' it became apparent that Churchward was about to embark upon a major transformation in locomotive design. Indeed by 1898 he

was fulfilling many of the duties of Chief Locomotive Superintendent, having received directorial instructions to make top level decisions. Dean's health continued to fail him but, out of respect for his long service, he was allowed to retain his position with Churchward fulfilling the role of 'regent'.

Between 1898 and 1899 a further batch of twenty 'Dukes' was produced. Fifteen had the round-top firebox as before but four carried boilers with Belpaire fireboxes

No. 2602, the second 'Kruger', is seen here at Evesham in 1903. These ungainly locomotives, which incorporated several advanced features, were not a success and the whole class was withdrawn by 1907. *Collection R. S. Carpenter*

An early 'Aberdare' 2—6—0 with a standard No. 2 boiler heads a lengthy goods train near Evershot on the Wilts, Somerset and Weymouth line.

similar to the 'Badmintons'. One, however, named *Bulldog*, carried a new design of boiler which was a turning point in GWR locomotive design. It was much larger and incorporated a longer Belpaire firebox than had been used previously. Although incorporating a dome, this was the prototype Standard No. 2 boiler, and three months after completion of *Bulldog* the last but one of the 'Badmintons' to be completed, *Waterford*, carried the second Standard No. 2. This second example had safety valves in the position previously occupied by the dome and with a Belpaire firebox, and the safety valves enclosed in a brass casing, this boiler was the first to include features that were to symbolise Great Western locomotives until the end of steam.

In 1899 a further attempt was made to produce an answer to the South Wales coal traffic problem. The result was another 4–6–0 No. 2601, but one which was of such outstanding ugliness that it was known to the enginemen as the 'Kruger', the Boer War having recently started. As with No. 36, it had inside cylinders, double frames and coupled wheels of 4 ft 7½ ins diameter. The first use of piston valves was accompanied by a number of innovative features which included a domeless boiler fitted with a raised Belpaire firebox casing, extended at the front to incorporate a combustion chamber.

In October of the same year a further batch of 4–4–0s with 5 ft 8 in coupled wheels appeared from Swindon, and the first of the class, *Camel*, was fitted with a domeless Standard No. 2 boiler and a drum-type smokebox. A new pattern of cast iron chimney was provided in place of the

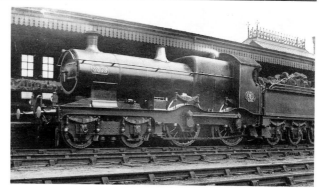

No. 3352 *Camel* at Gloucester when new. The smokebox mounted numberplate was an unusual feature not repeated elsewhere. *Collection John Lewis*

normal copper-capped steel chimney and for a number of years members of the class were known as 'Camels' although subsequently they became known as 'Bulldogs'. Initially, the new class had frames which curved over the axleboxes in exactly the same fashion as the 'Dukes', but following some experience with fracturing, from No. 3341, turned out in May 1900 onwards, the frames were given straight tops, thus giving additional strength between the coupled wheels. Most of the 'Camels' were sent to the West Country to assist the 'Dukes' and, indeed, took over from them on the more important expresses west of Newton Abbot.

An immaculately groomed 'Bulldog' No. 3445 *Ilfracombe* at Weymouth around 1906. For many years the 'Bulldogs' monopolised traffic on the Weymouth line, having taken over from the 'Dukes', until they too were superseded by 2–6–0s and 4–6–0s. *E. H. Seward*

'Atbara' No. 3379 *Kimberley* makes a spectacular exit from Kennaway tunnel, between Dawlish and Teignmouth, in the summer of 1904.

No. 3386 *Pembroke* was completed in August 1900 and this photograph, taken at Maidenhead, represents an 'Atbara' in its original, quite austere condition.
British Railways

In 1904 a 4–4–0 named *Atbara* with 6 ft 8½ in coupled wheels appeared from Swindon carrying a similar boiler to *Camel*. In fact *Atbara* bore the same relationship to the 'Badmintons' as did *Camel* to the 'Dukes' and henceforth the development of both 5 ft 8 in and 6 ft 8½ in double-framed 4–4–0s went hand in hand. The 'Atbaras' eventually numbered forty and were named chiefly after personalities or events connected with the Boer War. Their severe outline, so different from Dean's elegant machines, caused much controversy at the time of their introduction, but they soon developed a reputation for speedy running which silenced their critics and compensated for their looks. When first introduced, they were put on the same duties as the 'Badmintons', replacing the 4–2–2s on expresses between London, Bristol and Exeter and taking over from 2–4–0s on fast trains to Cardiff or between Bristol and Shrewsbury. They also worked on the Wolverhampton route which had only just been opened up to engines of this size and for a few short years early in this century the 'Atbaras' were the principal heavy express locomotives on the GWR.

Therefore, at the dawn of the new century the majority of trains were in the hands of locomotives of Dean design. Expresses were mostly worked by single-wheelers, some of which were less than three years old, assisted by increasing numbers of 4–4–0s with framing, cylinders, etc. of Dean design, but which above the running plate showed the influence of Churchward. The varying types of 2–2–2 and 2–4–0 tender engines were doing good work and were being constantly updated. Goods work continued to be handled by 0–6–0s, the most recent 'Dean Goods' having been completed as recently as 1897 but as yet there was no successful large replacement for the heavier work.

In August 1900 No. 33, a double-framed 2–6–0 with 4 ft 7½ in coupled wheels, was introduced and was, in effect, the goods version of the 'Bulldogs' and 'Atbaras'. Carrying a Standard No. 2 boiler, the engine was neat and compact compared with the 'Crocodile' and the 'Kruger' and was an immediate success. The locomotive was quickly followed by forty further engines and, as early members of the class were allocated to Aberdare, they became known as 'Aberdares'. Further engines were built with the Standard No. 4 boiler and in due course the earlier examples were brought into line, the class eventually numbering 81 locomotives.[1]

The following year a second 'Kruger', No. 2602, was produced and, as a result of the satisfactory design of No.

---

[1]   No. 33 was renumbered 2600 in December 1912.

For the first few years of the century the majority of main line goods work was in the hands of 0—6—0 locomotives as illustrated here by an unidentified 'Dean Goods' on the sea wall between Teignmouth and Dawlish.   *L & GRP, cty. David & Charles*

33, it was constructed as a 2—6—0. Inevitably the locomotive became known as 'Mrs. Kruger' and two years later a further batch of eight brought this class of very clumsy machines to ten. They were not a success as the boilers gave trouble, cylinders and motion were unsatisfactory and the crank axles were prone to failure. It seems that by attempting too many innovations, Churchward had overreached himself and by 1907 all the 'Krugers' had been scrapped. They were replaced by an equivalent number of 'Aberdares'.

Thus three classes, the 'Bulldogs', 'Atbaras' and 'Aberdares' were all running with the new Churchward boiler. Great care had been taken with its design and at the turn of the century the Standard No. 2 was probably the best boiler in Great Britain. The three classes incorporated double frames, which had practically been abandoned on all other railways, but the expense was considered worthwhile as the design allowed a much greater bearing surface on the driving axles. The GWR continued building locomotives of the type until 1910.

Also in 1900 a further departure from hitherto established GWR practice was made with the introduction of No. 11, a 2—4—2 tank with radial trucks at either end. Much used on the LNWR and Lancashire and Yorkshire Railway, the type was not common elsewhere and this novel engine incorporated an enclosed cab and water pick-up, both innovations on the GWR. The boiler was a shortened Standard No. 2 while the chimney and blast pipe arrangements were similar to the 'Atbaras'. No. 11 was put to work on local trains in the West Midlands.[2]

Apart from the double-ended radial tank, all of Churchward's designs produced during the 'regency period' were adaptations of Dean's practice and it was not until January 1901 that a drawing was prepared which indicated the way in which Churchward's mind was working. This showed that the production of double-framed engines was purely an interim measure until an entirely new range of locomotives could be worked out. The diagram gave outline specifications for six projected classes which were

2   No. 11 was renumbered 3600 in December 1912.

From 1905 the majority of 'Badmintons' received standard No. 4 boilers, thus making them the equivalent of the 'Cities'. No. 3305 *Samson* is illustrated in this form some time after 1909 when it was fitted with a copper-capped chimney, enlarged sandboxes and strengthened frames.   *L & GRP, cty. David & Charles*

This view of the cab of 'Bulldog' No. 3445 *Flamingo* illustrates the degree of standardisation achieved by Swindon. The various fittings and gauges, and their disposition about the backhead, were similar for a small tank or the largest 4-cylinder 4—6—0. Indeed the cab layout of this Edwardian locomotive would be very familiar to enginemen eighty years later.   *W. L. Kenning, cty. Adrian Vaughan*

The '3600' class was intended as an enlargement of the traditional 2−4−0T for suburban services. This view shows No. 3607 in original
condition.   *Collection J. E. Kite*

to be standardized in their form of construction with as
many parts as possible common to all types. All had
18 x 30 in outside cylinders, piston valves and all used
boilers of the same pattern. The six classes comprised two
4−6−0s, one for express work and the other for mixed
traffic, a heavy goods 2−8−0, a 4−4−0 for lighter express
work, a 4−4−2 tank for fast short distance work and a
2−6−2 tank for mixed traffic, suburban and general
branch line work. The coupled wheel diameter of the
express types was to be 6 ft 8½ in, the mixed traffic
2−6−2 and 4−6−0 5 ft 8 in, and the 2−8−0 4 ft 7½ in.
All these types were eventually built, although the mixed
traffic 4−6−0 did not appear until the mid 1930s in the
form of the 'Grange' class.

Of course this diagram was produced only for the
benefit of the GWR hierarchy, and to the outside world
the first tangible sign that something was afoot at Swindon
was when the 7 ft 8 in 'single' No. 3021 *Wigmore Castle*
travelled over every main line on the system fitted with
wooden templates attached to the outside frames between
the bogie wheels. The locomotive tested clearances to
check that outside cylinders would clear platform edges
and not foul the loading gauge, and great was the speculation amongst locomotive enthusiasts of the period.

When a few months later, in February 1902, a new
4−6−0 passenger engine appeared which was even more
stark and austere in outline than the 'Kruger' had been,
there was consternation amongst admirers of the GWR.
The locomotive, which carried the running number 100,

An unidentified '3600' class 2−4−2T with an eastern valleys
train from Newport around 1903.   *Collection Ian Cripps*

had inside plate frames, 18 x 30 in cylinders and a high running plate which exposed the driving wheels. Stephenson link motion was employed and reversing was by a long hand lever. The boiler was an enlargement of the 'Atbara' type, having a raised Belpaire firebox, safety valves on the parallel barrel and a drum type smokebox resting on a cast saddle. Much of the design followed contemporary American practice and the prototype GWR two-cylinder 4—6—0 might almost be termed an 'anglicised' version of the typical American 'ten-wheeler'.

No. 100 had a powerful vacuum brake applied to all wheels, including the bogie and tender, and this departure from previous practice was a result of the nasty fatal accident which occurred at Slough in 1900. At the resulting enquiry it was revealed that whilst the GWR vacuum brake was indeed more powerful than any in use by other companies, it was slow to operate, whereas a quicker acting brake might possibly have prevented the collision. Many experiments were subsequently carried out on coaching stock and a new design of vacuum cylinder was introduced. Churchward also issued instructions that henceforth all large express engines were to be fitted with the vacuum brake on all wheels.

In 1902 an event occurred which was to have important repercussions in the running of express trains on the GWR. In March the as yet uncrowned King

Two photographs of No. 100 *William Dean* the prototype Churchward 2-cylinder 4—6—0. The above view shows the locomotive, as refitted in 1903, with a standard No. 1 short cone boiler. The view below is of No. 100 at Taunton with its original, experimental boiler. Points to note are the non-standard pattern nameplates and the brakes fitted to the bogie wheels.

L & GRP, cty. David & Charles
and Collection J. E. Kite

'Atbara' No. 3408 *Ophir* in original condition at Kingswear around 1902. In 1907 this locomotive was rebuilt, with a standard No. 4 boiler, into a 'City'. In the same year its name was changed to *Killarney* on the occasion of the first Paddington-Killarney day excursion via Fishguard. Although intended as a temporary expedient, it never reverted to its former name.   *Collection Andrew Fiderkiewicz*

Edward VII and Queen Alexandra made a tour of the West Country, and with the monarch's well-known interest in scientific and engineering progress, it was suggested by the Great Western that the royal train should run the longest non-stop distance yet attempted by the company. To the King's delight, the train ran the 228.5 miles from Paddington to Kingswear without stopping. According to a contemporary report, it had been the intention to use No. 100 on this prestigious duty but in the event the train was hauled by the 4—4—0 'Atbara' class No. 3374 temporarily renamed *Britannia* especially for the occasion. On arrival at Kingswear the royal party crossed to Dartmouth where the foundation stone for the Royal Naval College was laid. Three days later, on 10th March, the return journey from Plymouth to London was similarly run non-stop although speed was reduced through Swindon to enable the workforce of some twelve thousand — almost the entire complement of the Locomotive and Carriage Works — to greet the King and Queen and to witness the passage of the elegant royal train. Clearly the Great Western was feeling its way with regard to non-stop running and further special trips were made which eventually led to the racing of boat train specials between

the GWR and LSWR and to the introduction of the 'Cornish Riviera Express' regularly running non-stop between Paddington and Plymouth.

At last, in May of 1902, Churchward succeeded William Dean as Locomotive Carriage and Wagon Superintendent. In June No. 100 was named *Dean* in honour of Churchward's former chief, the name being altered to *William Dean* in November 1902.

Development work on boilers continued and in the meantime further double-framed types of the 'Bulldog', 'Atbara' and 'Aberdare' classes were produced. The latest boilers incorporated a coned barrel and a tapered firebox, thus giving maximum cross-section at the firebox tube-plate. In September 1902 No. 3405 *Mauritius* of the 'Atbara' class was re-equipped with a new coned boiler classified as the Standard No. 4 and the locomotive thus formed the prototype of the famed 'City' class. Ten new engines followed in 1903 and nine 'Atbaras' were later rebuilt to the new specification.

The 'Cities' soon acquired a reputation for very fast running and in 1904 No. 3440 *City of Truro* was credited with a speed of 102.3 mph while working an 'Ocean Mails' special. Whatever one's views on the accuracy of the claim

This view of No. 3440 *City of Truro* was taken at Westbourne Park shortly after the locomotive entered service. Shown here in original condition, she is exactly as she appeared when the speed of 102.3 mph was achieved on an 'Ocean Mails' special from Plymouth to Paddington.

Collection R. C. Riley

there is no doubt that No. 3440's performance on this occasion was quite outstanding. Much was made in the contemporary railway press of the speeds attained by the 4—4—0s although news of *City of Truro*'s record-breaking run was deliberately supressed by the GWR authorities for fear of alarming the travelling public. In fact such was the company's desire to avoid any accusations of recklessness that it was many years before this performance received the recognition due to it.

However, the GWR was never slow to proclaim its own achievements and a paper delivered to the Great Western Railway (London) Debating Society by G. H. Burrows, Churchward's chief draughtsman at Swindon, contained a number of interesting facts. According to the paper, the running of the Plymouth 'Limited' and the special boat trains from Plymouth to Paddington during the summer of 1903 established for the GWR a number of records for regular running of high speed trains. A distance of 246 miles in a booked time of 265 minutes gives an average speed of 55.7 miles per hour from start to stop, a very

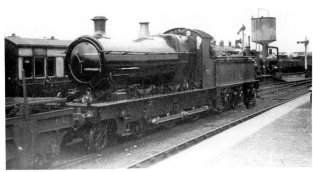

From the end of 1902 all new 'Aberdares' received standard No. 4 boilers and in due course earlier members of the class were brought into line. Recently modified No. 2642, in ex-works condition, is seen at Swindon Junction on a running-in turn.

L & GRP, cty. David & Charles

The second prototype 2-cylinder 4—6—0 No. 98 receives the attention of 'railwayacs' at Paddington when new. The locomotive was subsequently assimilated into the 'Saint' class. In 1907 it was named *Ernest Cunard* after a director of the GWR and the shipping line, and in December 1912 was renumbered 2998.

Collection J. E. Kite

high average for a regular service train whilst the distance run without stopping was unequalled elsewhere.

The paper further stated that such a long run had not been possible until water troughs had been installed in the permanent way every 40 to 70 miles or so along the route. A locomotive of the 'City' class was quoted as an example and it was shown that in the course of the long run from Plymouth to Paddington around 7,500 gallons of water were evaporated and 3¾ tons of coal burnt. With tenders of only 3,000 gallons capacity, water pick-up apparatus

frames. Although the bar frame arrangement was able to stand up to heavy shocks, its weaknesses were recognised, and overcome, to capitalize on the cheapness and simplicity of the cylinder arrangements that it allowed. Stephenson link valve gear was provided between the frames on all three prototypes, the motion being transmitted to the piston valve rods by means of rocking shafts.

While the prototypes had been under construction, spectacular work by the four cylinder de Glehn com-

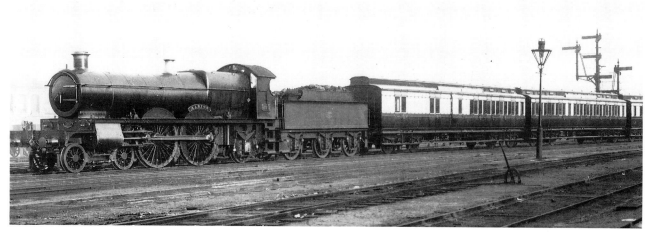

The third 2-cylinder express passenger prototype, No. 171, was soon modified to the 'Atlantic' wheel arrangement to provide a direct comparison with the 'Frenchmen'. This official photograph shows *Albion* at Swindon in this guise.   *British Railways*

was clearly essential in order that non-stop journeys might be sustained.

Following the undoubted success of the Standard No. 4 boiler with its greater steam-producing capacity, they were fitted to all the 'Aberdare' 2—6—0s built from the end of 1902 onwards, thus giving them a greater power output.

As remarked before, the continued production of double-framed engines was intended only as an interim measure, and the 2-cylinder 4—6—0 No. 100 indicated Churchward's thoughts in providing a class to take over the heavy trains from London to the West of England. Now he was fully in charge at Swindon, work in providing the GWR with a range of standardized, powerful, advanced locomotives continued. In 1903 three further prototypes were built, No. 98, a 4—6—0 passenger engine and a development of No. 100; No. 97, a 2—8—0 heavy goods engine and the first of its type in the country[3]; and No. 99, a 2—6—2 side tank locomotive for mixed traffic work. On all three of these engines further examples of contemporary American practice were to be found, particularly in the cylinders. Unlike No. 100, the cylinders consisted of two iron castings bolted back to back on the centre line of the locomotive and also incorporated the smokebox saddle and the steam and exhaust passages. To suit the arrangement of cylinders, American practice had to be followed for the framing at the front end. The main frames terminated immediately behind the cylinders which were carried by bar frames bolted to the main

pounds in France was attracting the attention of locomotive engineers everywhere. As Churchward was determined to provide the GWR with the finest possible locomotives, he recommended that the directors acquire a French 4—4—2 compound for an extended trial against his own engines. This was approved and on 19th October 1903 thirteen large packing cases containing the parts of the French 'Atlantic' which was to become GWR No. 102 *La France*, were landed at Poplar Docks. After erection and trials, it entered service during February 1904 and immediately started producing outstanding performances. The coupled wheels were of a size similar to No. 98 and the boiler was of similar dimensions to a Standard No. 1, although the working pressure was 227 lbs per square inch compared with 200 lb in Churchward's boiler.

To provide a more direct comparison, a further 4—6—0, No. 171[4], was built with a No. 1 boiler modified to a pressure of 225 lbs, a figure which henceforth became standard. However, as the 4—6—0 wheel arrangement offered a greater proportion of adhesive weight, No. 171 was built and subsequently modified to the 4—4—2 arrangement, by removing the trailing coupled wheels and adding a set of supplementary outside frames to carry the 4 ft 1½ in diameter trailing wheels.

While the trials between the express passenger locomotives were being made, further prototype locomotives

[3] Renumbered 2800 in December 1912.
[4] Named *Albion* in February 1904.

In 1903 the GWR took the unusual step of purchasing a de Glehn compound for comparative trials. Built by the Société Alsacienne des Constructions Méchaniques, at Belfort, the 4—4—2 was a replica of those built for the Nord Railway of France except for certain GWR requirements. The upper view shows the locomotive entering Paddington on an up express whilst the lower photograph shows No. 102 at Bristol Temple Meads in original condition. It will be noted that the engine carries a non-standard black livery, with red and white lining, and is paired with a standard 4,000 gallon tender.   *Ken Nunn/LCGB Collection and British Railways*

In September 1913 *La France* was altered to the form shown here, with superheater, top feed and new outside steampipes and the usual green livery.

British Railways

Although later known as the '45XX' class, the earlier members were numbered in the series 2161-2190, renumbering taking place in December 1912. This picture shows a recently completed member of the class working a passenger train in the Newport area.

Collection Ian Cripps

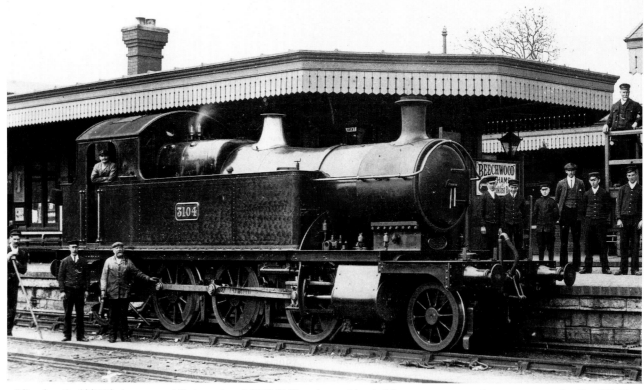

Likewise, the '44XX' class were at first numbered 3101-3110 and were identical in every respect to the prototype engine No. 115. No. 3104, later No. 4404, is shown here, in original condition, at Brent while working the Kingsbridge branch, a regular haunt of the class for many years.

L & GRP, cty. David & Charles

A 'County' 4—4—0 No. 3480 *County of Stafford* in original condition. The class was destined to be the shortest-lived of Churchward's designs — all had gone by 1933.   *P. W. Pilcher*

emerged from Swindon. The first, a small-wheeled 2—6—2 tank No. 115 which appeared in 1904, was intended for branch line work in the West Country. It proved entirely satisfactory and an order for further locos was placed with Wolverhampton works. However, as experience showed that larger coupled wheels would be beneficial, a further twenty were constructed at Wolverhampton between 1906 and 1908 with 4 ft 7½ in diameter driving wheels. Known as the '2161' and later '45XX' class, these twenty engines were the last to be constructed at Wolverhampton, all new construction henceforth being concentrated at Swindon.

A 4—4—0 with inside frames, outside cylinders and 6 ft 8½ in coupled wheels, also emerged in 1904. It was a shortened version of No. 98 and carried a Standard No. 4 boiler. No. 3473 was the first of ten locomotives of the type which, named after counties in England, Wales and Ireland, became known as the 'Counties'. Just why the 'County' class was built almost concurrently with the 'Cities' has long been the subject of speculation as both carried the No. 4 boiler and had 6 ft 8½ in coupled wheels. It was almost as if the 'County' was an assembly of standard parts simply for the sake of standardisation and the class was certainly the least successful of Churchward's designs. Furthermore, with a reputation for rough riding, they were the first Churchward type to disappear completely.

A further prototype which followed in 1905 was a tank version of the 'County' class. This 4—4—2 side tank was intended for short distance passenger work and had

a radial axlebox at the trailing end and water pick-up apparatus. The boiler was a Standard No. 2 rather than the No. 4 on the tender engines and, although unnamed, they were generally known as the 'County Tanks'.

It will be seen from the foregoing that by 1905 a range of standard types had been prepared and so advanced had Swindon's principles become that, after only limited experience with the first prototypes, batch production of subsequent new designs commenced almost straight away, the 2—8—0 and the 2—6—2 tank being the first to appear in quantity. The standard locomotives were assembled from a selection of components with a choice of four boilers and three coupled wheel diameters. Cylinders differed only in bore and it was only the frame arrangements which varied with each type. Parts common to all included piston rods, crossheads, piston valves, horn blocks, axleboxes, springs, valve motion and other assemblies including bogies, pony trucks and radial axleboxes.

With the almost constant stream of new types appearing, the attention of the contemporary railway press was continually drawn towards Swindon. Both professional and enthusiast journals reported on the performance and appearance of the new machines and the GWR, ever eager to foster and exploit any form of publicity, provided the necessary facilities.

1905 was a good year for enthusiasts (or 'railwayacs' as as the *Railway Magazine* termed them) and when The Railway Club visited Westbourne Park sheds, at that time still the GWR's principal locomotive depot in London, although soon to be superseded by Old Oak Common, the

No. 3476 *County of Dorset* at Bristol Temple Meads around 1906. With their short wheelbase and large outside cylinders they rolled badly at speed and earned the nickname 'Church-ward's Rough Riders'.

L & GRP, cty. David & Charles

No. 3479 *County of Warwick* shown here prepared for a Royal Train duty also displays an experimental tender insignia.

Collection R. S. Carpenter

In the renumbering scheme of December 1912 the earliest 'Counties' were placed in the '38XX' series. The second batch received the numbers 3801-3820 when new and No. 3817 *County of Monmouth* is seen here at Hereford Barrs Court around 1907.

Collection Rev. D. A. Tipper

Following the successful introduction of prototype No. 97, a batch of ten 2—8—0s numbered in the '28XX' series were introduced and revolutionised goods working. With only minor modifications, the class eventually numbered 168.   *Collection E. Mountford*

The '2221' class, also known as the 'County Tanks', were introduced for fast outer suburban working. This example, No. 2225, had the distinction, in 1909, of being repainted in an experimental crimson lake livery.   *L & GRP, cty. David & Charles*

Thirty-nine engines of the '3100' class were built following the introduction of the prototype No. 99. No. 3141 is shown here in original condition in the Newport area.   *Collection Ian Cripps*

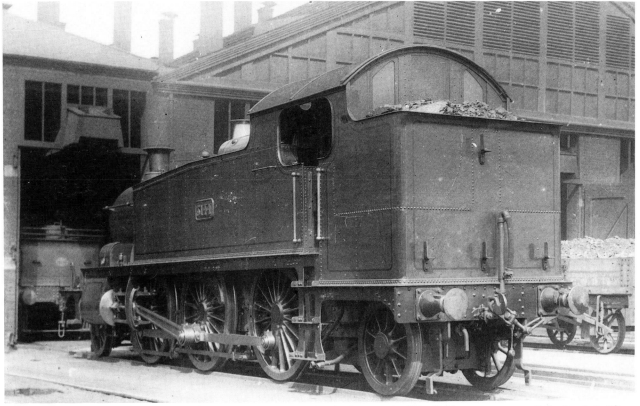

The 2—6—2Ts were extremely high-standing locomotives as shown in this photograph of No. 3144.   *Collection J. E. Kite*

A Dean 'singlewheeler' negotiates the approaches at Paddington with an up passenger train. Enthusiasts of the period would have had a perfect vantage point from the platform ends of the wonderful variety of motive power to be seen at the company's London terminus.

Collection J. E. Kite

guide was no less a person than Mr. W. A. Stanier. Among the locomotives noted during the visit was the 4–4–0 *Earl Cawdor* with its immense boiler. A unique 2–8–0 was examined, its massive proportions exciting universal attention and in the repair shop 4–4–2 *Albion* was under inspection.

Individual enthusiasts were also able to observe the GWR at work and Paddington was an ideal place to do so. The noted railway historian J. N. Maskelyn spent a day there taking photographs in 1905 but, although the Churchward engines were in attendance, his attention was drawn to the older locomotives facing relegation to secondary duties or even scrapping. Among the high spots of the day was the arrival of the 2–2–2 No. 165 on a special from Oxford carrying academics. She returned to her home shed in the afternoon piloting an 'Atbara' 4–4–0 on a Birmingham train. Other locomotives noted on that occasion included 2–4–0 No. 807 on a train for Reading, a similar engine No. 817 on a Weymouth train, 'Barnum' 2–4–0 No. 3224 on a West of England express and 2–4–0 No. 76 *Wye* on the afternoon Trowbridge train. 'JNM' saw several of his favourite class, the Dean 7 ft 8 in 'singles', No. 3040 *Empress of India*, No. 3044 *Hurricane* and No. 3076 *Princess Beatrice* on an Oxford train of very mediocre stock.

2–2–2 No. 165 entering Oxford on a down passenger train.
L & GRP, cty. David & Charles

No. 3297 *Earl Cawdor* with the large experimental boiler and Churchward cab. The boiler was taken off in 1906.
L & GRP, cty. David & Charles

Like No. 102, 'Frenchmen' Nos. 103 and 104 were also built at Belfort but were similar to the Paris-Orleans Railway examples. No. 104 *Alliance* is shown in original condition.

Collection John Lewis

After two years' experience with No. 171 *Albion* and the French compound No. 102, it was found that there was little to choose between the two. No. 102 was smoother running at speed and was expected to run a greater mileage between overhauls. It was felt that wider experience was necessary and it was decided to purchase two more de Glehn compounds. These were larger and when delivered in 1905 were numbered 103 and 104 and named *President* and *Alliance* respectively. In the same year, and to compete with the new arrivals from France, a further nineteen locomotives of the same type as *Albion* were constructed at Swindon. Thirteen emerged as 4–4–2s and the remaining six as 4–6–0s. The 'Atlantics' were particularly fine looking machines and their names, taken from the novels of Sir Walter Scott, suited them well.[5]

It became obvious as the trials continued that not only was the question of compounding against simple expansion to be settled but also that of 4–4–2 versus 4–6–0. However, by 1906 further experience with the three French compounds clearly defined the next step. Churchward's engines, with their high boiler pressure and long valve travel operated by Stephenson link motion, were just as economical on coal consumption as the de Glehn compounds and he obviously felt there was nothing to be gained by adopting the additional complication of compounding. However, the French engines gave much smoother running with their balanced reciprocating masses due to the four cylinders, and it was felt preferable to divide the drive between two axles instead of one.

The result was a further 4–4–2 locomotive No. 40 which carried a Standard No. 1 boiler, wheels of the same diameter as the two-cylinder 4–4–2s, and plate frames throughout. A pair of outside cylinders overhung the rear bogie wheels and drove on the second coupled axle, while the inside cylinders were placed well forward and drove on the leading coupled axle. The valve gear presented something of a problem in that there was insufficient

room for the usual Stephenson link motion, and an unusual form, known as 'scissors gear', was adopted and situated between the frames.

In service No. 40, soon given the name *North Star*, fully realised Churchward's objective of combining the best of Swindon and French practices. It was soon proved beyond doubt that compounding was of no advantage under running conditions but it was felt by the operating staff that a 4–6–0 would be preferable as its greater adhesive weight would be invaluable on heavily graded sections of the line such as in South Devon. It was, therefore, decided that the two-cylinder 4–6–0 should be considered the normal express passenger type, and the 4–4–2s were consequently converted to suit. However, there was also a requirement for a limited number of four-cylinder 4–6–0s for heavy non-stop express work running at high speed and therefore a batch of ten four-cylinder

No. 104 at Bristol Temple Meads in 1907 after being fitted with a standard No. 1 boiler.   *L & GRP, cty. David & Charles*

[5] All the 4–4–2s were converted to 4–6–0s between April 1912 and January 1913.

No. 104 *Alliance* at Paddington some time between 1907 and 1908 when it carried a standard No. 1 boiler. The locomotive had brought in empty carriage stock from Old Oak Common yard which would form a later departure. No. 104 would then have taken its place at the head of a subsequent train, the stock of which will have been brought to the terminus by either a 'pilot' or another express locomotive running tender first.   *British Railways*

Following the successful introduction of No. 171 *Albion*, in 1905 a further nineteen 2-cylinder engines numbered 172-190 were built, thirteen as 4—4—2s and the remainder as 4—6—0s. This view shows No. 179 *Magnet* at Bristol Temple Meads. The locomotive was renamed *Quentin Durward* in 1907, was converted to a 4—6—0 in 1912 and renumbered 2979 in December of the same year.

L & GRP, cty. David & Charles

As well as working west of England trains, the class also worked to South Wales. No. 186 *Robin Hood* is seen here at Newport High Street in 1908.　　　　　　　　　　　　　　　　　　　　　*G. M. Perkins*

Not all of the batch were named at first and No. 182 is seen here in original condition. In 1909 the name *Lalla Rookh* was allotted to the engine.　　　　　　　　　　　　　　　　　　　　*Collection R. S. Carpenter*

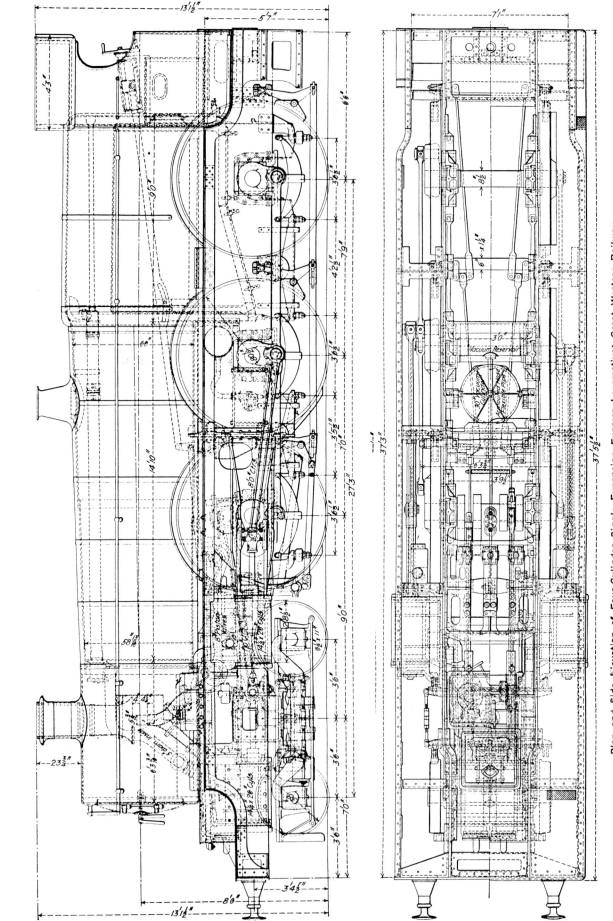

Plan and Side Elevation of Four-Cylinder Single Expansion Express Locomotive; Great Western Railway

No. 40 emerged from Swindon in 1906. Later it received the name *North Star*, a name famous in GWR history, and was converted to a 4−6−0 in 1909.

British Railways

4−6−0s was ordered. Numbered 4001 to 4010, they were given the names of the early broad gauge single-wheelers of 1839-41 and thus was born Churchward's immortal 'Star' class.

The 'Stars' emerged from Swindon during 1907 and their appearance was much improved over No. 40 by having the drops on the footplate framing curved at both ends. Walschaert's valve gear was adopted for this batch and all subsequent four-cylinder engines, and screw reversers were fitted as standard.

Immediately on introduction to service, it was realised that the GWR had an exceptional class of locomotive. The contemporary railway press published many journey logs which were intended to show the superiority of the 'Stars' over other companies' express locomotives and the general concensus of opinion was that a 4-cylinder simple 4−6−0 engine was the type best suited to maintain high speeds with heavy loads. One particular article made comparisons with the Hughes locomotives of the same configuration on the Lancashire and Yorkshire Railway. They were turning in good work and interestingly (considering their present day reputation) the Drummond 4-cylinder simple 4−6−0s of the LSWR were said to be doing quite well on the heavy summer traffic to the west. However, the 'Stars' quickly proved to be quite outstanding and many reports appeared of the prodigious loads worked while still maintaining schedules. On 30th July 1909, for example, No. 4005 *Polar Star* took the 1.00 p.m. two-hour express to Bristol out of Paddington loaded to no less than seventeen eight-wheelers, and workings of this nature were by no means the exception. Concurrently with the 'Stars' a further batch of two-cylinder 4−6−0s was built. These were named after 'Saints' and eventually the entire class of '29XX' 4−6−0s came to be known by this name. After the four-cylinder engines had been in service for a while it was possible to compare the performance of them against the equivalent two-cylinder

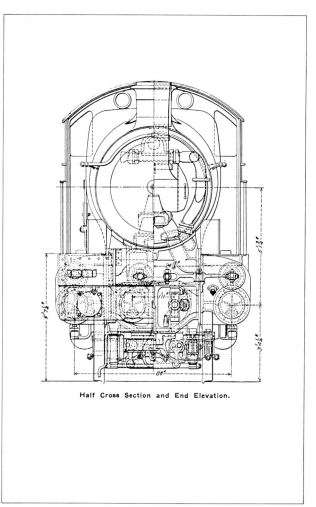

Half Cross Section and End Elevation.

A drizzly day at Paddington as No. 4017 *Knight of the Black Eagle* is prepared to take a special train to Newbury.

No. 4006 *Red Star*, seen here in original condition at Ashley Hill, exhibits the clean lines of Churchward's masterpiece.

L & GRP, cty. David & Charles

The complete Churchward train. An unidentified 'Star' at the head of a train of 70 ft 'Dreadnought' coaches.   *Collection John Lewis*

No. 2903 was built in 1906 and is seen here when ex-works in the full splendour of the pre-war finish. She received the name *Lady of Lyons* in 1907.

British Railways

No. 2921 *Saint Dunstan* at Bristol Temple Meads in original condition. The 'Saints' were built in 1907 and in due course the entire '29XX' class was known by this name. The framing incorporated the curved ends at front and rear, a feature that was found on all subsequent GWR 4—6—0s.

L & GRP, cty. David & Charles

The imposing front aspect of the '29XX' class is seen to advantage in this view of No. 2926 *Saint Nicholas*.   *E. Pouteau*

This view at Old Oak Common shows a 'Saint' at the head of a vacuum fitted goods train whilst 'Dean Goods' locomotives carry out shunting duties.
Collection R. C. Riley

machines. It was the opinion of the locomotive inspectors that the 'Stars' were 'a coach better' with trains of 12 or 14 vehicles running at 60 mph or over, but at lower speeds the two-cylinder engines had the advantage of faster acceleration.

Just as the new 4—6—0s transformed express running, so the introduction into service of numbers of the '28XX' 2—8—0 wrought considerable changes in goods and particularly mineral working. Once the potential of the class had been realised, the traffic department were quick to take advantage and increased the number of wagons per train. As soon as the loops and sidings between Swindon and London had been lengthened, loads were substantially increased until a maximum of 100 wagons, representing a total of 1,600 tons, was reached. Shorter distance goods work was similarly transformed by the 2—6—2 tanks.

Additional express goods and perishable trains were introduced in 1905 running from Acton to Bristol and, as an increasing amount of vacuum-braked rolling stock came into service, new train services were introduced covering most main line and cross-country routes. These trains, loaded to between 40 and 60 continuously-braked vehicles, ran at an average speed of 35 mph. Passenger engines were used to work them and, with double-framed 4—4—0s generally being used, further batches of these engines appeared from Swindon in 1906.

By 1903 the railways came increasingly under threat from electric tramway operators which were competing for the lucrative traffic in city suburban areas. However, so far as the GWR was concerned, the decision to adopt steam railmotor cars seems to have been in response to a Stroud District and Cheltenham Tramways Bill. The

Great Western, ever watchful for threats to any traffic monopoly, countered with a proposal to introduce a new service of stopping trains, using railmotor cars, between Gloucester, Stonehouse, Stroud and Chalford. The LSWR were the innovators of this novel form of vehicle and, after a brief trial period when the South Western 'car ran on the GWR, two railmotors numbered 1 and 2 were built at Swindon. They inaugurated the long-lived railmotor service in the Stroud Valley and within five years the GWR was by far the most prolific user of these vehicles.

Typically, the GWR turned this defensive action into a publicity campaign, claiming proudly that it was the company's intention to bring train services to the smallest communities throughout the system. Not only was the steam railmotor car seen as the railway company's answer to the threat of the electric tramcar in the cities, but also to the motor 'bus in country districts. The construction of 'halts' (or 'haltes' in contemporary parlance), small stopping places with minimum facilities, enabled this policy to be applied with the minimum outlay and 145 were opened prior to the outbreak of war in 1914.

The railmotor consisted of a carriage body mounted on bogies, one of which was the power unit which incorporated a vertical multi-tubed boiler and Walschaert's valve gear. The coach body was of the open saloon type and had a driving compartment at the trailing end equipped with regulator, brake valve and bell communication to the footplate. Ninety-nine cars were built, mostly at Swindon, but a number were supplied by contractors to several different patterns depending on the service for which they were intended. Vehicles were built to work suburban, main line and branch services. More power units were

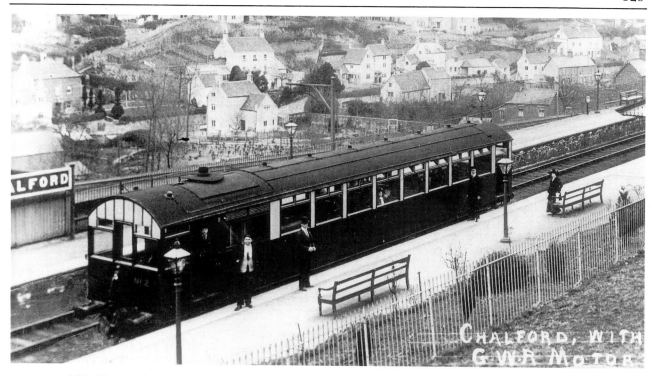

Two views of the first GWR railmotors at work in the Stroud Valley. The upper photograph shows No. 2 at Chalford with the driving compartment windows modified to improve vision. The lower view shows one of the cars at Ebley Crossing Halte shortly after the service commenced. At this early stage the stopping place consisted of little more than a patch of gravel and a notice board. Access to the car from ground level was by the steps at the end of the vehicle. *Collection Gerry Beale and Collection H. G. W. Household*

Later cars retained the flat matchboarded sides of the original pair but had angled ends as illustrated by No. 3 when working from Southall to Brentford.

Collection Paul Karau

provided than the number of cars, the majority being constructed at Swindon although a few were provided by Wolverhampton.

In service the cars performed well and, where gradients permitted, a trailer or two could be added at times of peak traffic. They were even used for shunting at country stations and could commonly be seen trailing a number of horse-boxes or even goods wagons. Although in some cases the railmotors arrived too late to prevent traffic transferring to the roads, in other instances they were so successful and generated so much extra traffic that they had to be replaced. They also had several disadvantages in

No. 69, shown here at Campden on the Oxford, Worcester & Wolverhampton line, was built in 1906 and illustrates the third, and more familiar body style of these vehicles.

Lens of Sutton

The first GWR auto-train at Southall. The Armstrong '517' class No. 1160 is painted in a 'chocolate and cream' livery to match the trailer coach but the cream painted cab and toolbox did not remain this colour for long!

British Railways

Two of the auto-fitted '517s', Nos. 533 and 833, were encased in dummy coachwork to match the trailer-cars. One is seen here at Trumpers Crossing Halte on the Southall-Brentford branch.

Collection R. S. Carpenter

servicing as the entire unit had to go to locomotive sheds and, quite apart from the room that they occupied in shed yards or repair shops, all coaling had to be done by hand, and the paintwork and seating was liable to be soiled by dust and smoke. Therefore in 1905 the auto-train was introduced.

Consisting of a small tank locomotive hauling or propelling one or two coaches, these most individual of Great Western trains were an immediate success. The auto-cars were adapted from the steam railmotor trailers and included the driving compartment as before. A system of rodding, with universal joints and couplings, was connec-

could do well it was decided to equip the best of them with a new pattern of domed Belpaire boiler and to scrap the rest. Thus it was that the single-wheelers continued to provide useful service until December 1915 when the last two, Nos. 3050 *Royal Sovereign* and 3074 *Princess Helena*, were withdrawn. They were the last single-wheelers to run on the GWR.

In January 1908 a massive new locomotive of the 4—6—2 'Pacific' type appeared from Swindon. It was the first of this wheel arrangement to be built in Great Britain but the reason why Churchward decided on the construction of this enormous machine has remained an enigma

Six-coupled tanks were also clad in dummy coachwork. An example is illustrated here in company with four 70 ft long auto-trailers probably for working in the Plymouth area.
British Railways

ted to the regulator of the locomotive, along with the brake valve and bell communication. The locomotives used were almost all of the Armstrong '517' class 0—4—2Ts, with 5 ft 2 in coupled wheels, although a few of the '2021' 0—6—0Ts with saddle tanks were also used. The auto-trains were well within the capabilities of these locomotives and extra carriages could be added at peak times whilst, in addition, the locomotive could be released for servicing or even used on other duties.

In certain areas, notably Plymouth where an intensive service was operated between the rapidly expanding suburbs to the east and west of the city, the auto-trains consisted of four 70 ft long trailer vehicles with the loco-motive sandwiched in the middle of the train. But it was considered that the presence of a locomotive in this most unusual position might be the cause of some concern to passengers and so (and possibly to satisfy some curious Edwardian aesthetics) a few of the 'auto-engines' were enclosed in dummy coachwork. Consisting of thin steel platework shaped to match the carriage profile and painted in the same chocolate and cream livery, the enclosed locomotives were not liked by the operating staff and the coachwork was removed in 1911.

By 1907 it was becoming difficult to find sufficient work for the 80 single-wheelers of the 'Achilles' class. Increasingly heavy train loadings limited their usefulness but Churchward seemed reluctant to scrap them, the newest examples being only eight years old. Since the turn of the century domeless Belpaire boilers had been fitted to some until the class was subdivided into two. Churchward's first proposal was to convert them to 4—4—0s but this was soon found to be hopelessly uneconomic. As there was still some work which the engines

Above shows No. 2120 in ex-works condition whilst below is No. 2140 unclothed at Laira.
British Railways
and W. Beckerlegge

Not a 'Star' but a 'Constellation'! *The Great Bear* at Paddington in 1908 in original condition. Although Churchward is said to have had a dislike of the 'Pacific' it was highly successful as a publicity exercise.
Collection Gerry Beale

and over the years several theories have been mooted. One was that Churchward received directorial instructions from the GWR Board to produce the largest engine in the country simply as a matter of prestige. Whilst Churchward warned the Board that the locomotive would be costly to produce, and be restricted in its use, it is possible that he welcomed the opportunity to build a four-cylinder locomotive that would be even more powerful than the 'Stars'. Churchward could already foresee the time when the 'Stars' would be stretched, and even more power required. He probably also welcomed the opportunity to experiment with a wide firebox similar to that used on Ivatt's highly successful 'Atlantics' for the Great Northern Railway.

With running number 111 and named *The Great Bear*, what emerged from Swindon was a locomotive that was basically a 'Star' in so far as the frames, cylinders, wheels, motion and bogie were concerned. A radial truck was provided at the rear to accommodate the trailing carrying wheels. It was the large boiler which was the principal feature of interest in the new machine, with a wide Belpaire firebox and 23 ft long barrel made up of three rings, one of which was coned. A special tender was also provided running on a pair of locomotive type bar-framed bogies.

Whilst the appearance of *The Great Bear* certainly brought much prestige to the GWR, in service the locomotive was something of a disappointment. She showed no advantage over the 'Stars', which were well able to cope with the longest trains that the platforms at Paddington could handle, and her axle-loading restricted her sphere of operation. For this reason she was limited to the London-Bristol main line, working passenger and vacuum-fitted goods trains. She developed a rather shaky reputation amongst the running staff and had an annoying habit of derailing herself on the approaches to Paddington's departure platforms when backing onto trains and for this reason was banned from using Platform One.

Concurrently with the construction of *The Great Bear*, further batches of 'standard' locomotives were built

including twenty 2—6—2 tanks of the '3150' class, ten more of the 4—4—2 'County' tanks and ten more 'Stars'. A further twenty double-framed 4—4—0s with 6 ft 8½ in coupled wheels were also built. Known as the 'Flower' class, they had Standard No. 2 boilers, instead of the No. 4 of the 'Cities', and were intended for working on secondary routes. They were closely followed by fifteen more 'Bulldogs' of the 'Bird' series which were the last double-framed locomotives to be built anywhere in the world. Construction of this outmoded pattern continued because Churchward had been concentrating on providing the main lines with suitable up-to-date motive power and he was still undecided about what he would do for secondary routes. However, these services urgently

In 1908 a final batch of double-framed 4—4—0s with 6 ft 8½ in driving wheels emerged from Swindon. No. 4102 *Begonia*, seen here at Platform 1 at Paddington, was renumbered 4150 in 1912.

L & GRP, cty. David & Charles

LNWR 'Experiment' class No. 1471 *Worcestershire*, on a down train to Plymouth, passing Subway Junction during the 1910 locomotive exchange. The first vehicle in the train is the Dynomometer Car No. 790 whilst a Hammersmith and City line electric train can be seen emerging from beneath the main line *en route* to Hammersmith.

Cty. LNWR Society

required new locomotives due to the demise of the early, and now outdated, 2—4—0 and 2—2—2 tender classes.

During the last year of the decade under review a further prototype locomotive appeared from Swindon. Containing as many 'standard' components as possible, the new machine was a 2—8—0 side tank engine, almost a tank version of the '28XX' 2—8—0, intended for use in South Wales when there was a requirement for a loco-

was selected to oppose her. No. 4005 *Polar Star* went to the LNWR where she ran against No. 1455 *Herefordshire*.

On the GWR *Worcestershire* performed badly. Much time was lost, coal consumption was heavy and finally the engine failed at Exeter on her last down journey. On the LNWR *Polar Star* was complete master of the trains she worked and with a smaller coal consumption than the competing 'Experiment'.

No. 4005 *Polar Star* at work on the LNWR.

Ken Nunn/LCGB Collection

motive capable of working short distance heavy mineral traffic. To allow the engine to negotiate sharp curves, additional side play was allowed in the trailing wheels. It was fourteen months after the appearance of No. 4201 that further examples of the type appeared, when a batch of twenty were built.

In 1909 Churchward was coming under mounting criticism in the contemporary engineering press regarding the high cost of GWR locomotives compared with other companies, especially the LNWR. Locomotive running costs were also questioned, particularly as the apparently cheaper LNWR machines were capable of taking heavy trains over the notorious Shap incline. Churchward was obviously keen to prove his point as he proposed that a locomotive exchange be effected to see how the two companies' engines compared in service.

The arrangement was that for two weeks in August 1910 an 'Experiment' class 4—6—0 of the LNWR should run on the GWR and a 'Star' on the North Western. Apparently this period was chosen by Churchward in order that the 'Star' might display its capabilities when working heavy holiday expresses but the timing had an unfortunate effect on the LNWR performance. When Camden shed was advised to send an 'Experiment' to Old Oak Common they sent the locomotive which they could best afford with dire results! LNWR No. 1471 *Worcestershire* duly arrived on the GWR and No. 4003 *Lode Star*

It has often been stated that the LNWR 'Claughtons' were built as a result of the trials but according to O. S. Nock in *The Great Western Railway in the 20th Century*, this was not the case. As related earlier, it was already accepted by locomotive engineers that a 4-cylinder simple 4—6—0 was the best machine for fast, heavy, express train working, and no doubt the LNWR Chief Mechanical Engineer, C. J. Bowen-Cooke, was pleased enough to have

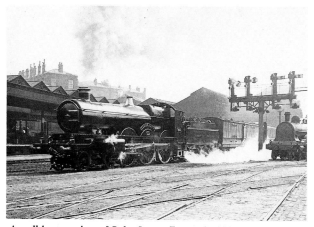

A well-known view of *Polar Star* at Euston in 1910.

British Railways

One of the first '43XX' 2—6—0s working an up goods train through Abingdon Road Halt, south of Oxford, early in the Great War. This halt opened in February 1908 when an Oxford area railmotor service was inaugurated, but lasted only until March 1915.

W. L. Kenning, cty. Adrian Vaughan

a 'Star' available for his personal inspection, but the proposed North Western engine would not include Swindon's distinctive and expensive features. When, in 1913, LNWR No. 2222 *Sir Gilbert Claughton* emerged from Crewe, the 4-cylinder 4—6—0 locomotive had a superheated boiler and the class proved to be the ultimate express locomotive built by the company.

As far as Churchward was concerned, his locomotives were completely vindicated and after the trials there were no further questions as to their expense.

In early 1910 there was much speculation in the railway press regarding the forthcoming opening of the Ashendon-Aynho line over which the GWR proposed running two-hour expresses from Paddington to Birmingham. The Great Western was making an attempt to gain a portion of the lucrative passenger business between the capital and Britain's second largest city, but in so doing were competing directly with the LNWR and, to a lesser extent, the Midland Railway. However, the LNWR, which styled itself the 'oldest established firm in the passenger business', proved to be a much more energetic competitor than had been the LSWR in the West Country, and even before the GWR route was open, had not only improved

the frequency and timing of its service but also provided new rolling stock.

When the GWR commenced its Birmingham service on 1st July 1910 the Press run maintained the two-hour schedule precisely in the down direction, but on the return to London the train left Snow Hill no less than seven minutes late, although it was only ½ minute down at Paddington. A rather cynical observer at Paddington on the first day reported that most trains from Birmingham were arriving between 7 and 10 minutes late and as they consisted of between four and seven eight-wheelers, the weight of the engine exceeded two-thirds that of the train weight!

Causes of the delays were given as severe permanent way slacks at various points along the line and excessive station time at Leamington. In time the slacks were eased as the road bed settled down but it is unlikely that the locomotives were hard-pressed with such lightweight trains over an easily graded and generously engineered route. Only Hatton bank presented any obstacle and this was not considered to be a particularly fearful impediment to the modern Churchward engines. Apart from the rather lack-lustre locomotive performances on the Birmingham services, the object of most comment was the low standard of carriage stock provided. The usual GWR mixture of types was in evidence and, although modern elliptical-roof vehicles were under construction at Swindon, it was considered a grave error not to have had new stock available for the commencement of the service.

By 1910 Churchward decided that he had completed his programme of 'standard' types for main line work and at last turned his attention to providing locomotives for use on secondary routes. He did not wish to perpetuate the double-framed engines of the 'Atbara' and 'Bulldog' types, although he wanted to retain inside cylinders on inside-framed locomotives. This was soon found to be impracticable and in 1911 there appeared a class of outside cylinder 2–6–0s with 5 ft 8 in diameter coupled wheels carrying the Standard No. 4 boiler. These locomotives were almost the tender version of the '3150' class 2–6–2 tank, and were something of a milestone in British locomotive history, being the first general utility locomotive. The '43XX' was an immediate success, indeed no prototype was built, a batch of twenty being constructed straight away. Further examples were built and they served with distinction during the Great War, a number being requisitioned by the Army and sent to France. Eventually the class numbered some 342 examples.

By now Churchward was satisfied that he had provided the GWR with the locomotive types necessary to operate all traffic on the system and it was anticipated that subsequent new construction would be of existing standard types. Nine designs were considered to be the 'standard' classes. They were the 4–6–2 express engine, of which *The Great Bear*, although a one-off, was included because of the aforementioned affinity with the 'Star' class, the four-cylinder 4–6–0 'Star' class for long distance expresses, the two-cylinder 4–6–0s of the 'Saint' class, the two-cylinder 4–4–0 'Counties' which worked passenger trains on the LNWR/GWR joint line from Shrewsbury to Hereford, and elsewhere in the Northern Division, the 4–4–2 'County Tanks' for fast London suburban services, the large 2–6–2 tanks for short distance mixed traffic duties, the 2–8–0 heavy goods engine, the 2–8–0 tank for short haul heavy mineral work and the 2–6–0 mixed traffic locomotives. The small wheeled 2–6–2T was not considered to be part of the standard range, but it earned its place through sheer merit and during the 1920s the numbers of this type were greatly increased.

Although the range was now considered to be complete, work was constantly in progress on updating the locomotives and in particular their boilers. An important provision was the addition of top-feed and since 1906 experiments had been underway with superheating. Various patterns were tried with the result that the Swindon No. 3 superheater was adopted. Fitted initially to express passenger and heavy goods classes, in due course the entire range of 'standard' classes and many locomotives of Dean and Armstrong design were equipped.

In the years after 1910, until Churchward was succeeded by C. B. Collett in 1921, two more 'standard' engines appeared. No. 4600, a 4–4–2 tank with 5 ft 8 in wheels, was introduced in 1913 and was intended for working passenger trains in Cornwall. However, it was found to be no improvement over the successful '45XX' tanks and the design was not repeated. Later, following the Great War, a large 2–8–0 locomotive with 5 ft 8 in coupled wheels emerged. Numbered 4700, it was intended to be a heavy mixed traffic type and an improvement on the '43XX' 2–6–0s. It included some features from *The Great Bear* and a further eight were built in 1922-23. Although they were successful, on the night-time express goods services, on which they were employed, their weight and lengthy wheelbase restricted their range and so no further examples were built. It was not until 1924 when Collett rebuilt No. 2925 *Saint Martin* with 6 ft diameter coupled wheels that an effective improvement over the '43XX' was produced. Even so, the Running Department had to wait until 1928 before the first batch of the widely acclaimed 'Halls' appeared from Swindon.

As Locomotive Carriage and Wagon Superintendent (in 1916 the title of the office was changed to Chief Mechanical Engineer) Churchward was responsible not only for the design and manufacture of locomotives but also for the running and maintenance of the machines in service. Servicing and repair facilities were provided at various locations throughout the system and, although a degree of standardisation had been achieved during the time of William Dean, in the period under review Churchward implemented many improvements New designs were prepared, not only for shed structures but also for repair shops, coaling stages and even track layouts, which followed a standard form and varied only in accordance with local requirements.

The first of the new Churchward sheds was Old Oak Common which opened in 1906 to replace the old broad gauge shed serving Paddington at Westbourne Park. At the time of its construction it was claimed to be the largest in the world. The main shed building, which could accommodate 112 locomotives, measured 360 ft by 444 ft and contained four 65 ft electrically operated turntables. It is evident that when preparing the design Churchward adopted the modern principle, then fully recognised in the USA, of carrying out the major proportion of repairs required by locomotives at district sheds, thus rendering unnecessary the frequent visits to central repair shops. At Old Oak Common a lifting shop was provided which, accommodating up to twelve locomotives under repair, was equipped with an overhead electrically-operated crane and, outside the building, an electric traverser. Electrically powered machine tools were provided in quantity and a compressed air plant supplied power to many pneumatic tools used in the shop. There were well-appointed smiths, coppersmiths and carpenters shops along with a comprehensive stores, messrooms and office accommodation for the chief running shed foreman. A separate block of offices was provided for the London Divisional Locomotive Superintendent, Mr. John Armstrong.

When the shed opened, the allocation of locomotives at Old Oak Common was 154, of which 83 were passenger engines, the remainder being used for goods working. Of course engines from other sheds were serviced there while waiting in London between journeys.

Largest and grandest of Churchward's locomotive sheds was Old Oak Common which opened in 1906. This view, taken shortly after, shows the enormous coaling stage and water tank with two locomotives in attendance, a Dean 2—4—0 No. 2206 and a Churchward 'Atlantic' No. 190 — later 4—6—0 No. 2990 *Waverley*.

British Railways

Tyseley was built later than Old Oak Common and on a slightly lesser scale. *British Railways*

The spacious interiors of the Churchward roundhouses revolutionised working conditions for the shed staff. The new shed at Tyseley is seen here in 1908 before the allocation arrived. *British Railways*

A final line-up at Old Oak Common with locomotives of Churchward origin at last gaining the ascendancy over Dean's designs. Engines visible are 'County' No. 3811 *County of Bucks* and an unidentified 'Saint', Dean '2201' class 2—4—0, and a 'Star'.

Collection R. C. Riley

As well as roundhouses, a new design of straight shed was adopted. Opened in 1907, Severn Tunnel Junction was later enlarged by the addition of a third bay accommodating two extra roads. *British Railways*

The extensive use made of electric power both for operating machinery and lighting was of particular note in the railway press. At the time this was considered to be most progressive. Current was drawn from a nearby GWR power station, recently built in connection with the electrification of the Hammersmith and City Railway.

Old Oak Common was considered to be the model of its kind in 1906 and, although similar sheds were built elsewhere on the GWR system, none approached it in size. Eight turntable sheds and nine straight road sheds were eventually built to Churchward's design and, but for the Great War, doubtless others would have been constructed to replace older buildings.

As well as the updating of running sheds, Churchward implemented many important improvements at Swindon. As early as 1895 he had noted the inadequacy of the facilities at the works and, as related earlier, Wolverhampton was proposed for expansion as the major locomotive works of the GWR. However, there were difficulties in acquiring land at Stafford Road and so instead Churchward recommended the construction of a new workshop on the area of land at Swindon which had initially been acquired for the reception sidings for redundant broad gauge stock. What was eventually built became the famous 'A' shop, an extensive structure capable of handling the construction and repair of the large number of modern locomotives which emerged from the works in the years up to 1914. The construction of this shop, incidentally, marked the final ascendancy of Swindon over Wolverhampton in locomotive matters.

Churchward ensured that the new shop was equipped with the most modern machinery whilst an unusual feature was the construction of a locomotive testing plant. Not intended originally for experimental or research purposes, although this was no doubt an additional consideration, its primary purpose was the 'running-in' of new or newly repaired locomotives, so saving track occupation on the congested double track through Swindon. In this it was not entirely successful and not much used for the purpose. Testing was carried out with

the assistance of the dynamometer car, No. 790, built in 1901.

It will be seen from the foregoing that in the years from 1900 to 1910 Churchward introduced substantial reforms throughout the Chief Mechanical Engineer's Department. Of course, many were already in progress before the turn of the century and they continued, perhaps less dramatically, until 1914 when railway developments everywhere were halted by the outbreak of the 'Kaiser's War'. During this first decade the standard classes were created and developed and for a few years at least the GWR possessed the most modern fleet of locomotives, serviced and repaired in some of the most well-appointed running sheds and workshops in the country. Sadly, by the 1930s the company began to fall behind and the publicity department had to work overtime to keep the GWR in the public eye against the glamorous streamliners of the LMS and LNER. The degree to which they succeeded is witnessed by the high esteem in which the company is still held today, but in truth by nationalization Swindon still largely followed the principles of Churchward which, by 1948, were decidedly dated. However, the writing was clearly on the wall for steam traction everywhere and there seemed little point in making major changes. Thus the revolutionary changes made early this century lasted for around sixty years, a fact which Churchward surely could not have foreseen.

Apart from the aforementioned Holcroft book, this account leans heavily on Colonel H. C. B. Rodgers' biography of Churchward, Alan Peck's history *The Great Western at Swindon Works* and the RCTS *The Locomotives of the Great Western Railway*. Magazine articles in *The Engineer* and *Railway Gazette* were consulted as well as period enthusiast journals, *Railway Notes and the Locomotive Review, Locomotives and Railways*, and, of course, *The Railway Magazine*. My thanks are due to John Kite, Roger Carpenter, Chris Turner, and in particular Chris Hawkins for curbing my worst excesses of Great Western jingoism!

'Victorian elegance' — the only expression for this train. A Dean Single heads a train of matching 8-wheeled clerestory coaches. Come the Churchward revolution and things would never be like this again. The locomotive is *Majestic* and the train the 10.35 Paddington to Penzance, photographed near Bath in August 1899. The coaches were built for the 'Cornishman' train in 1893 and have side gangways. The last coach is a slip.

British Railways

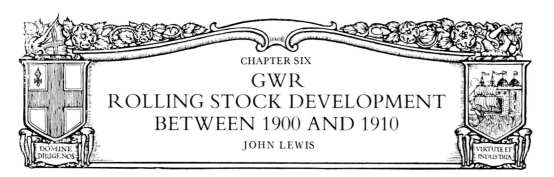

CHAPTER SIX
GWR
ROLLING STOCK DEVELOPMENT
BETWEEN 1900 AND 1910
JOHN LEWIS

DURING the first decade of the twentieth century there were considerable changes in rolling stock design on the GWR. The 'Churchward Revolution' manifested itself throughout the Great Western so far as locomotives and rolling stock were concerned, although with Churchward himself busily engaged in the provision of the 'standard' locomotives, it is probable that developments at the Carriage and Wagon Works were largely in the hands of subordinates. In many ways this revolution might be thought of in terms of economies of scale, with larger coaches and wagons, as well as 'Stars', 'Saints' and 2–8–0s, and this had considerable benefits for both passengers and other customers. It was, moreover, the era when many types of rolling stock adopted a 'modern' guise, the resulting designs with only relatively minor modifications, often being perpetuated up to, and indeed beyond, the end of the GWR.

The clerestory-roofed eight-wheeled coaches introduced on the broad gauge in 1876 were not the earliest eight-wheeled passenger vehicles on the GWR — there had been the 'Long Charlies' — but they were the first of the standard clerestory designs that were built until 1904. In time, versions were also built for the 'narrow gauge' (i.e. standard gauge) and gradually they started to replace low roof four- and six-wheel short coaches.

Over the years there were some developments in coach design, but they were relatively small; roof profiles changed from a plain arc to 3-arc (known as 'elliptical'), the low windows and deep eaves panels changed via some transitional designs to tall windows and shallower eaves panels, and external coach widths increased during the 1890s from 8 ft 0¾ in. on standard gauge stock to 8 ft 6¾ in. Guards' compartments normally had projecting look-outs to enable them to see down the length of the train without putting their heads out of the windows. These look-outs were characteristic of the period and the narrow gauge coaches where these present measured some 9 ft 3 in wide over them. They are known variously as 'wings', 'projections', 'ogees' or even 'OGs'.

In 1879 comfort for a very few 1st class travellers was significantly increased when water closets and washing facilities first appeared in ordinary carriage stock, initially in eight-wheel broad gauge examples. What our Victorian forebears called 'lavatories' were wash basins, which is why some sleeping cars were able to boast 'folding lavatories'! However, they did not become usual until 1884 and even then only selected first class compartments in eight-wheel stock had access to them. WCs for passengers travelling third class did not appear until about 1890, and

again usually only in the larger coaches. A long distance journey in those days required considerable forethought!

Fortunately trains then tended to stop more frequently and for longer than they do nowadays. For example, in 1886 the 11.45 a.m. express train from Paddington to Penzance stopped at Swindon for 10 minutes, Bristol for 5, Taunton for 4, Exeter for 10 minutes (from 4 p.m. until 4.10), Newton Abbot for 5 minutes and at Plymouth for another 10. It eventually arrived in Penzance at 9.00 p.m. The stop at Swindon was in fulfilment of the GWR's contract with the proprietors of the refreshment rooms and passengers had ten minutes to eat a meal, see to their personal comfort . . . and regain their seats on the train.

Gangwayed stock made its first appearance on ordinary passenger trains in 1890-2, and then only experimentally. A few postal vehicles had been equipped with this facility for some time and, like the postal vehicles, the coaches concerned had side gangways which meant that they could not be connected if the coaches had been turned round relative to each other. These pioneer gangwayed coaches were built in what was known as the 'bay window' style because they were 8 ft 6 in wide externally at the doors (with one door to each compartment) bowing out to 9 ft wide between them. Otherwise they were very similar in appearance to contemporary clerestory stock. More gangwayed trains were produced for the main line services to and from Paddington, but it was a slow business. By the summer of 1894 the GWR had six trains formed of gangwayed stock, one each to and from Birkenhead, Penzance and Kingswear.

Restaurant cars appeared on the GWR in 1896 when three were built along with two clerestory passenger brake vans with kitchens, followed by a 'kitchen brake first' in 1897. Their introduction was the result of the GWR buying out the lease of the Swindon Refreshment Rooms in October 1895 when it still had some 45 years to run. The new vehicles enabled trains to run through Swindon without stopping for the first time. The restaurant cars were initially all first class only, and they were easily recognisable by the almost square-shaped windows of the dining saloons, the lack of side doors and by the clerestory roof which had sloping sides, although some sleeping cars also shared these features.

Normally passengers travelled in their compartments for the whole of the journey, and if they wanted a meal they travelled all the way in the restaurant car. They were not encouraged to use the gangways which were for the use of the guard. Some coaches were equipped with an electric alarm system by which he could be summoned (if

A GWR clerestory restaurant car (nearest the camera) and a 68 ft corridor brake tricomposite at Barnstaple. The brake was a unique design built at the transition between the clerestory coaches and Churchward's modern designs.   *L & GRP*

it was connected up!). Otherwise, in an emergency, there was a cord running the length of the train suspended through rings below the coach gutter *outside* the coach, and if this was hauled on sufficiently it would sound a whistle or a bell on the locomotive. From 1896 gangway connectors were positioned centrally on the coach ends, instead of being offset, and from 1897 the corridor had large windows extending between adjacent doors instead of pairs of quarterlights. From 1898 corridor gangwayed coaches became the norm for new main line passenger carrying stock.

For long distance cross-country traffic to and from other company's lines and for through traffic to branch lines, non-gangwayed brake tricomposites were built, and some of these were constructed as slip coaches. The latter had apparatus to enable the guard to detach the vehicle from the main train and to bring it to a halt at an intermediate station at which the main train did not stop. In these coaches the brake compartments were at the end of the coach and, although in some vehicles there was only one such compartment, many slip coaches were double-ended. There was an end window for the guard to view the line ahead and a slip lever, normally padlocked out of use, which enabled the guard to uncouple the slip portion from the main train and simultaneously apply the brakes.

However, it was not quite this simple for, according to the 1905 issue of the General Appendix to the Rule Book, the guard had to operate a valve on the last coach of the main train. Quite how was not made explicit, but he had to operate a special valve on the brake pipe, presumably reached by opening the window at the end of the slip coach. He then had to operate a valve in his own coach, thus sealing the brake pipes of the main train and the slip portion. With this done he made a light application of the handbrake of his coach and then pulled the slipping lever which actually released the slip portion from the main train. Finally, he was expected to stop the slip portion in the correct place using only the handbrake. The vacuum brake was for use in emergencies as once it had been applied it could not be released, there being no means of restoring the vacuum. Consequently, the slip guard was a highly skilled man with a responsible position.

In the 1891 GWR Rulebook, rule 60A provided that where the main train carried only one slip portion, then the last carriage of the slip should carry the usual red tail lamp with an additional lamp placed vertically above it. During the day, each of these lamps was 'to be encircled by a disc painted the same colour as the light shown at night'. If the train conveyed two slips, then the portion to be slipped first (i.e. the last coach(es) of the train) should carry on its rear a *green* lamp above the red tail lamp, again circled with discs. The second portion to be slipped carried two vertical red lamps as above. In addition to these lamps, each slip carriage had to carry the usual two side lamps.

This only provided for a train to convey a maximum of two slip portions at any one time, but by the summer of 1894 the 8.20 a.m. Birkenhead to Paddington was regularly, if not frequently, carrying three slip tricomposites as it left Birmingham Snow Hill. One was slipped at Knowle on the 'third Wednesday in each month'(!), one at Hatton and a third at Warwick. These coaches were all liable to be six- or even four-wheeled vehicles.

By 1905 it had been decided that a green light on the rear of a train was not good practice and the instructions were altered so that where there was only one slip portion, the last carriage carried a white lamp adjacent to the red tail lamp. If there were two slip portions, then on the first to be slipped, the white lamp was placed vertically below the red tail lamp. The second portion to be slipped carried the horizontal arrangements of these lamps. The rules regarding encircling discs still applied, as did the requirement for the slip portions to carry the usual side lamps. A new instruction required the leading carriage of the slip to carry a white headlamp after dusk, in foggy weather and during falling snow. This was placed on a special lamp bracket next to the droplight in the end of the carriage. The possibility of a third slip portion was still not recognised.

In 1909 the GWR modified the slip apparatus to make control of the slip portion simpler for the guard. The improvements consisted of valves to be fitted (specially) to the slip coach and the last coach of the train so that the brake pipe was automatically sealed when the pipes were parted. The action of the slip lever was modified so that it partially applied the vacuum brake to the slip portion before the actual slip took place. In addition, extra vacuum tanks were now carried on the slip coach which were connected to the vacuum brake pipe by valves. These were arranged so that when the train first started they had the air exhausted from them and they were then disconnected from the vacuum pipe by a non-return valve (otherwise they would reduce any braking effort applied in the normal course of the train's running). When the slip had been made, the guard could push his slip lever right forward again and the vacuum tanks would be connected directly to the brake pipe, thus releasing the brake, and the slip portion would then coast freely. Further brake applications could be made by the guard in this way, but the vacuum tanks would eventually become ineffective as their vacuum was lost in releasing the brakes. The number of times a guard could release the vacuum brake in this fashion varied with the number of coaches (more accurately, with the number of brake cylinders) on the

A two coach portion for Windsor being slipped at Slough. The slip coach was one of a pair built for through services from the GWR to the SECR. They were slipped at Reading on the southbound journey although these particular vehicles may not have been actually used on this service as they were closely followed by another pair, without the guard's look-outs. The rear Windsor coach is one of the oldest designs of clerestory with deep eaves panels and low windows.   *British Railways*

slip portion, but if there was only the slip coach he could probably do it four or five times.

The modern slip coaches with their high roofs carried the additional vacuum tanks transversely on the underframe, whilst the clerestory slip coaches had long tanks mounted on the main roof on either side of the clerestory. Here they remained, often long after the coach had ceased to be used as a slip coach and had had the rest of the slip apparatus removed.

In due course the rules were revised yet again, certainly by 1920 and possibly in 1909, when new slip apparatus was introduced. The last carriage of the main train carried a special double red tail lamp which showed two red lights arranged vertically. The lamps on the slip portions were as in 1905, but if there were three slip portions then the first portion to be slipped carried a triple tail lamp which showed a white light to the *left* of the red tail lamp, with another red light above. The longest use of the triple tail lamp was probably the winter 'Cornish Riviera' with slip portions detached at Westbury for Weymouth, Taunton for Ilfracombe and Exeter for Kingswear.

In spite of the hazards and costs of slip operation, which required a senior guard to every slip coach and special arrangements to get the vehicles back to their starting points, the GWR was quite keen on their use. The use of slip coaches reached a peak in 1910-1914 and they continued, albeit on a decreasing scale (excluding both World Wars when their use was not permitted), for the remainder of the GWR's existence. The last did not take place until well into BR days, at Bicester in 1960.

Through coaches, including slip coaches, continued to be developed during the 1890s and were eventually standardized on a scheme involving (usually) at least one guard's compartment, a couple of 1st class compartments with a lavatory each (modern use of the term) sandwiched between them, one 2nd class compartment also with its

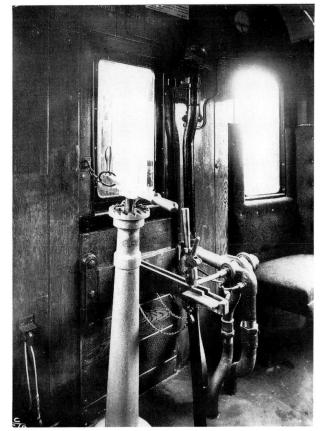

Interior of guard's compartment of a slip coach. This is the 1909 improved mechanism. Note the interlocking of the brake pipe and the slip lever. Nearest the camera is the handbrake.   *British Railways*

Late Victorian GWR stopping train, still oil-lit. These coaches would have been built as main line stock in the 1870s or 1880s and are shown at Bewdley shortly before the turn of the century.

Chambers Collection, Kidderminster Museum

In some ways this was a traditional GWR train — no two adjacent vehicles matching. The coach nearest the camera looks like an ex-Bristol & Exeter vehicle of 1875/6; the next is a GWR centre brake third of 1876-82 and probably an 8-wheel brake composite of 1888 or later. Note the difference in height and roof profile between the two GWR coaches and the broad gauge clearances between the tracks. This picture was taken at Marsh Mills c.1900.
Collection H. F. Wheeller

own lavatory, and up to five 3rd class compartments connected by a side corridor and served by two lavatories, one for ladies and one for men. The corridor was internal only and did not serve the first or second class compartments and all compartments had their own external doors. Some of these through coaches had observation windows in an end first class compartment. Rather strangely, in spite of most of these coaches having 'wings' to the guard's compartments, they seem to have enjoyed wide acceptance by other railway companies unlike the slightly longer 9 ft 3 in wide stock of later years. One coach with wings actually brought down part of a footbridge at Crewe station in 1900 when a handle attached to the outside of the wing came in contact with one of the footbridge's supports. The LNWR asked the GWR not to send this type of coach to Crewe again.

In due course, around the First World War, it was decided that five lavatories were generally too many for a single coach and one of those for the use of third class passengers was removed. It had usually been occupying space which would otherwise have been the guard's compartment.

The GWR had introduced first class only sleeper services in 1877, the coaches involved, two 6-wheel vehicles 29 ft long and 10 ft 6 in wide, operating over the broad gauge between London and Penzance. These coaches effectively had two dormitories, one with seven beds for men and the other with four for ladies. There was no lavatory. Not surprisingly, these particular coaches were not over popular and were replaced by 8-wheel vehicles in 1881. The new coaches provided for a greater degree of privacy, although all the compartments were either twin or three berth, involving not bunks but proper beds!

The history of the earliest GWR sleeping carriages is too involved to go into here, but by 1900 there were

services to South Wales as well as to Penzance, operated by six coaches that now included composite sleeping cars. These vehicles had first class sleeping accommodation, and second and third class compartments with ordinary seats, the GWR not introducing third class sleepers until 1929.

Thus at the commencement of the century the GWR had about 150 gangwayed general purpose clerestory coaches available, three 1st class dining cars and three other coaches with kitchen facilities and six sleeping cars for the best main line services to and from London. Less important trains had non-gangwayed stock, but at least a proportion had access to toilet facilities. Most new coaches were 54 ft to 58 ft long, 8 ft 6 ins wide, although 40 ft x 8 ft in eight-wheel low roof passenger brake vans were still under construction as were four-wheel coaches for local services. At this time most of the through main line trains presented a uniform appearance that was rarely achieved in later years.

As always, there was a strong tendency for the newest and best coaches to be allocated to the most prestigious main line services to and from Paddington. Although stock was still being built new for local and stopping services, older and smaller vehicles were regularly displaced onto stopping main line services and branch line trains, the oldest stock being withdrawn from those services. Stopping trains were generally a mixture of older and more modern 8-wheel clerestory and low roof coaches, and four- and six-wheelers of all vintages. However, by 1900 the last of the old 7 ft 6 in wide flat-sided coaches were almost extinct.

The London local services included trains to and from the City via what is now the north side of London Regional Transport's Circle line. There were severe limitations on the length of trains on this line and special coaches had been provided since the 1870s, particularly noted for the poor standard of accommodation which was

Wolverhampton. This shows the 'elliptical' roof of a clerestory composite coach nicely. This coach, Diag. E33, was built in 1891/2. Only two of the three 1st class compartments had access to a W.C. There was a luggage compartment (the double doors) so it would have been built for main line work. 8 ft wide coaches had five end panels, like this one, and 8 ft 6 in wide ones had six. At the extreme right there is a slip coach.

G. M. Perkins

This ten-coach train approaching Bathampton is probably an excursion of some kind, or possibly a workmen's as all the coaches are 3rd class, with one possible exception. The leading clerestory coach is a rather magnificent 8-wheel brake 3rd of 1885 (Diag. D3). Note the arc + arc roof and deep eaves panels. Next come four low single arc roof thirds (6-wheel) with 5 compartments, a 4-compartment coach of similar style which may be a 1st, 2nd or compo, an elliptical roof all third (notice it is slightly taller), two more arc roof 3rds and a centre brake third. The arc roof 6-wheel 3rd was a design built from 1873 to 1884. The elliptical roofed one was a 'modernised' version of the same.

L & GRP, cty. David & Charles

Acton with a nice train of matching 4-wheel close-coupled suburban coaches. They date back to 1880 or even earlier, but here they are gas-lit with flat flame burners. Nearest the camera are two seconds, then three firsts. The last two coaches may be third class. These coaches tended to be displaced by the later design 'Metro' vehicles which were 8 ft 6 in wide and had the distinctive curved tops to the doors. Note the class designation is in large numerals on the doors. The 2nd class were merely better upholstered thirds!

Collection R. S. Carpenter

very cramped. From the 1880s the doors were given semi-circular tops with matching ventilators, which gave these coaches a distinctive appearance and kept them within the loading gauge should a door accidentally open in a tunnel. By 1900 many of the older 'Metro' coaches were in the process of being relegated to provincial services and replaced by new stock of similar appearance. Some trains of these older coaches went to the Birmingham Division.

At the start of the new century two important changes were underway. Coach lighting was being changed from oil to gas and, quite literally with one or two exceptions only, this was complete by 1910 so far as passenger carrying stock was concerned. Only horseboxes and fruit vans retained oil lighting, and did so for many years to come.

It must be remembered that in 1900 the development of electric lighting for moving trains was in its infancy and the light from the new incandescent gas burners was often better than that from electricity. Another advantage of gas over electricity was that it did not involve drag from a dynamo, a factor that was important at a time of rising train weights and the common use of 4–2–2 'single-wheeler' express locomotives with their inherently limited adhesion. Compared with oil, both systems gave much improved illumination but they both involved increased coach weights due to gas cylinders, or batteries and dynamos. With the primitive state of battery technology at 1900, gas was probably lighter, but required plant to produce it, (already built) special gas holder wagons to transport it, the cylinders needed charging frequently and the gas mantles in the incandescent burners were fragile

and needed regular replacement. The biggest disadvantage of gas lighting was the fire risk, but the accidents at Ais Gill on the Midland Railway and at Quintinshill on the Caledonian Railway were some years into the future.

The second major change was the provision of steam heating in all new passenger vehicles and the equipping of much of the older stock. By the period under consideration, third-class passengers had been allowed glazed windows for quite some time and a roof over their heads for somewhat longer. But the trains themselves remained completely unheated and, given the state of technology in the earlier years of the 19th century, the thought of flexible pipes carrying live steam is better not considered.

However, to lessen the suffering of the upper classes travelling first-class, footwarmers had been introduced in 1856. Consisting of an oblong tin filled with hot water, they were changed at principal stations along the line, but in the case of expresses to the south-west, this meant at Bristol, Exeter and Plymouth, which gave plenty of time for both passenger and footwarmer to cool down. In 1870 the privilege was extended to passengers travelling second-class and in 1873 reluctantly to third-class passengers. There matters rested until November 1891 when the new corridor train was equipped with steam heating. This was gradually extended to other coaches, new main line stock having priority as usual.

In January 1896 Churchward read a paper on 'Modern Railway Carriages' to the Junior Engineering Society of the GWR Mechanics' Institute in which he described the system, apparently pioneered by the GWR, whereby compartments were heated by steam pipes looped round under the seats. The steam flow could be regulated by the driver and by a guard if the leading carriage had a guard's compartment. There were originally thermometers in the coaches for the guard's benefit, but passengers became partial to them and they disappeared. Pressure in the heating system was limited to 60 lbs/sq. in. by a relief valve on the locomotive's tender. This pressure was used only when heating a train from cold, as in normal running 20 lbs/sq. in. sufficed in cold weather and 10 lbs/sq. in. in mild winter weather.

There were two principal problems in arranging a steam heating system of this kind — condensation in the pipes and flexible connections between carriages. Condensation was dealt with by a system of drain pipes and drain valves, the latter arranged so that they let water out without allowing steam to escape. By 1896 Churchward was able to report that agreement had been reached between the railway companies as to a standard coupling for steam pipes between coaches and an example was shown in his paper where it is described as a 'Westinghouse coupling'. In order that condensate should not block the steam pipe, the couplings each had a thermostatic drain valve as part of the fixture.

In 1896 other railway companies employed similar systems to the GWR to heat their carriages but, according to the paper, they differed by using 'Storage Heaters' instead of plain pipes for the heating elements. These storage heaters consisted of a branch pipe enclosed within a larger one, and the space between the two pipes was filled with sodium acetate or brine to act as the storage medium. The advantage of the GWR's system was that their heating pipes comprised a continuous series of loops under the seats whereas the rival systems used terminating branch pipes. The GWR system also involved the heating pipes being inset into the floor of the carriages, except under the seats where they were above the floor, whereas other systems had the main steam pipes below the floor, presumably for safety reasons, but at the cost of heat loss.

Progress in providing steam heating is perhaps best described as 'steady' during the later 1890s, although, according to the carriage lot list, five 4-wheel brake thirds were built in 1901 *without* steam heating. Nevertheless, by then footwarmers had largely dropped out of use although they could still be ordered until 1908.

In 1900 the GWR built five coaches for the Paddington-Milford Haven boat train service. These were notable because they were the first general purpose stock on the railway to have electric lighting, although the 1897 royal train had also been equipped with it. In addition, they were the first coaches on the Great Western with the internal communication cord system operating on the vacuum brake pipe, a system still in use today. This resulted from experiments carried out by the Manchester, Sheffield & Lincolnshire Railway from about 1890 and was generally adopted by all railways, with the blessing of the Board of Trade, around the turn of the century. The new communication cord was introduced fairly rapidly and incorporated in existing coaches, but electric light took longer and not many coaches were converted from gas.

The Milford boat train coaches, together with another set built the following year, were what we would term today 'open' coaches. The GWR called them 'centre corridor' stock and the adoption of this design was possibly another example of Churchward importing ideas from abroad. This seating layout was used almost exclusively in the USA but on the GWR the coaches were unpopular with passengers travelling to and from Ireland and the boat trains were normally supplemented with a conventional compartment composite vehicle.

In October 1901 HM Treasury agreed that the overnight Paddington-Penzance mail train, the Great Western TPO, should become a 'special' mail train, i.e. it would no longer convey fare-paying passengers. This took effect from 1st January 1902, the trains consisting of clerestory-roofed mail vans, low roof passenger brake vans and four rather smart clerestory passenger brake vans. These last included two with kitchen facilities, the company therefore being left with five normal restaurant cars, 2 buffet seconds for the Milford trains, passengers now being permitted to use the gangways, and no less than eight of the rather curious brake first kitchen and brake third kitchen cars, seven of which had been built in 1900.

Gangwayed passenger-carrying coaches continued to be built in quantity, about 100 being constructed during 1900-2.

One particularly interesting coach was built in 1902. Numbered 2400, it was a standard clerestory gangwayed brake third — except that it was no less than 68 ft long — and was a portent of things to come on the GWR. Although an experimental design and not repeated, it nevertheless must have shown that long coaches were a practical possibility, and it survived with relatively minor modifications until February 1950.

1902 saw the last four-wheeled passenger coaches built and 1903 continued the mixture much as before, another sixty or so clerestory gangwayed coaches being built, amongst them four composite dining cars with seats for all classes of passengers. The existing first-class diners were altered to composites.

However, probably the most important rolling stock development of 1903 was the introduction of two steam railmotors on the Chalford-Stroud service. Following trials on that line with a railmotor owned jointly by the LSWR and LBSCR, which was normally used on the East Southsea (Portsmouth) service, the GWR design was considerably more powerful and had a four coupled 'power' bogie as opposed to a 'single driver'. The first GWR railmotors had an open saloon for the passengers, with a driver's compartment at each end, and the vertical boiler in its own compartment between the saloon and a driving compartment. The boiler was totally enclosed within the bodywork of the vehicle and only the chimney, just visible above the roof line, and the cylinders and motion on the power bogie would have identified it as anything other than an ordinary coach to the casual onlooker.

In outline these coaches were unusual for the GWR in having a high elliptical roof and flat sides with vertical matchboarding below the waist. The latter feature appeared on relatively few of the earliest railmotors and

Steam railmotor No. 7 at Resolven. This matchboarded style of side panelling was only used on the first few steam railmotors and on one trailer. (See also pages 123 *et seq.* and 189 *et seq.*)
Lens of Sutton

on only one of the trailers. The later steam railmotors and trailers were built with turn-under sides with conventional wood panelling until in later years it was superseded by metal sheeting. The first two steam railmotors had flat ends, but all subsequent vehicles and their trailers had very pronounced angled ends. Another new departure for the GWR, and one which was to become standard on all steam railmotors and trailers, was the use of hinged toplights above the large windows of the passenger saloon.

The railmotors were an immediate success and generated increased traffic, helped in some instances by the building of unstaffed halts or 'haltes', as they were then known. Some of these platforms were initially no more than sleepers placed alongside the track adjacent to a suitable level crossing, and the railmotors and later trailers were equipped with steps, suspended beneath the passenger's door, which folded back out of the way when the train was running. Another twelve steam railmotors were built by the end of July 1904, these being of a similar appearance to Nos. 1 and 2, but having the angular bow-ends as mentioned above.

Following on from construction of the first two steam rail motors, a matching trailer carriage appeared in December 1904. This coach had a driving compartment at only one end and was designed to run with a steam railmotor and was built in the same style. As already mentioned, this particular trailer remained the only one of this pattern until the early steam railmotors were altered to auto trailers. Of greater significance were the trailers numbered from 2-6 which were built between December 1904 and April 1905. These were 70 ft long and 9 ft wide and were panelled like an ordinary coach. They had the same high elliptical roof as the steam railmotors.

The most interesting feature of these vehicles was that they were primarily intended to run with a locomotive

and they introduced the era of locomotive-worked push and pull trains that was such a feature of the GWR. In practice there turned out to be a number of advantages in using the auto train concept rather than simply using a steam railmotor. The initial cost of a trailer was significantly less than a comparable steam railmotor, as much as £700 or 50%, this difference being largely caused by the cost of the engine unit.

The engine unit of a steam railmotor was really quite low powered when compared with a locomotive, although the GWR's were better in this respect than many contemporary examples. They were sufficiently powerful to accelerate from rest to 30 mph in about 30 seconds when running solo, a fact aided by their small driving wheels, 3 ft 6 in or 4 ft, and they had a top speed of about 45 mph. However, there were real limitations on the amount of tail traffic that they could handle, which was normally no more than two coaches. In addition, the GWR had available a number of 0−4−2 tank engines that otherwise would have been redundant and these were suitable for work with trailers.

As a combination of locomotive and coach, the steam railmotor had some inherent problems, most notably its need to visit locomotive facilities in order to take on coal and to be serviced. It was hard to keep the passenger accommodation clean in such circumstances and in addition, should the engine develop a fault, then the whole vehicle was out of action. The design of most of the GWR steam railmotors meant that removing the engine unit was a major task requiring lifting facilities.

The theoretical advantage of the steam railmotor over the auto train, was its lower running costs and the lower initial cost if taking the locomotive into account. It was possible for the GWR to avoid this by using old, fully depreciated locomotives for auto train work, and it was

Newnham in 1910 and the classic GWR auto-train, in this case the Cinderford branch train headed by 0—4—2T 564 of the '517' class with two trailers.
British Railways

not until the 1930s that purpose-built motive power was provided for these services.

The operating rules for auto train working laid down that a maximum of two trailers could be propelled but this restriction did not apply to tail traffic, which was limited only by the power of the locomotive. Where three or four coach trains were required it was the practice to marshall a locomotive in the middle of the train, and, to avoid frightening nervous passengers who would not be expecting an engine in this position, some were even clad to look like a coach.

Steam railmotors were built until 1907 by which time there were 99 of them. Conversion to trailers started in 1915 and was not completed until 1936. There were some 75 trailers by 1910 and they continued to be built well beyond the end of the GWR.

The next event to catch the railway press headlines occurred in 1904 when a new dining car appeared carrying the number 1575. This massive vehicle was yet another Churchward prototype and within twelve months further examples were built. In 1906 they received the nickname of 'Dreadnoughts' after a recently completed battleship which had rendered all previously built capital ships, including those of the Royal Navy, obsolete. Amongst other features HMS *Dreadnought* was notable for a dramatic increase in size over previous ships and in the same way the GWR took full advantage of the generous

loading gauge of ex-broad gauge lines with these magnificent vehicles. No. 1575 was 9 ft 6 in wide; it had a high elliptical roof which gave an internal clearance of 8 ft and was 68 ft long. The dining saloons had large windows each with hammered glass toplights hinged downwards to provide ventilation, a feature of GWR dining cars until the mid 1930s. It also had fixed toplights above the droplights and other windows, another feature of general purpose GWR coaches until the end of World War I.

Internally the coach had a centre kitchen with a first-class saloon at one end and another for passengers travelling second- or third-class at the other. There were vestibules across the coach at each end and these had flat access doors that were significantly recessed from the coach sides which were of the normal turn-under profile. These distinctive recessed ends made passenger-carrying 'Dreadnought' coaches easy to recognise. No. 1575 was electrically lit using Stone's system, like the Milford boat train coaches, and with few exceptions electrical lighting became standard for new passenger stock henceforth. The alternative electric lighting system used by the GWR was the Lucas 'Leitner' system and in time this became by far the most common in use by the company.

The pioneer 'Dreadnought' was followed by others of the same style comprising dining cars, thirds, brake thirds and composites, most being electrically lit from new. New features for general purpose main line coaches were the limited access, the corridors which changed sides at the central vestibule, and the non-opening toplights above all windows. Many features of the diners were incorporated in the ordinary coaches: the wide and tall bodies, the long length (between 68 and 70ft) and the cross vestibules, which were placed at both ends and at the centre of the coaches, although the central doors were not recessed as much as the end ones. One advantage of this arrangement was that it permitted the use of longer members in bodywork construction, and, so far as passengers were

In size, the 'Dreadnoughts', and in particular their width, caused some quite severe operating restrictions. Not only would no other railway company allow them over their system, but even on the GWR they were largely confined to ex-broad gauge lines. Thus they could be used only between Paddington and Penzance, both via Bristol and via Lavington when that route was opened, and in South Wales they were effectively confined to the main line between Paddington and Swansea, Milford Haven and Fishguard. They were not allowed north of Hereford on

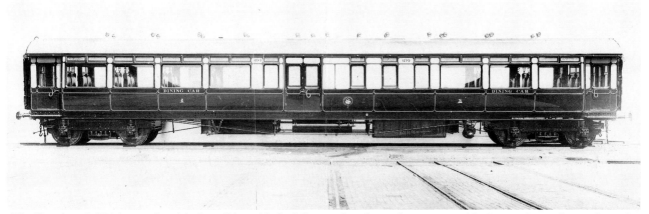

The 'Dreadnought' Dining car. In original condition with the full two colour livery, they were arguably the most impressive coaches built by the GWR. *British Railways*

concerned, meant that there were no draughty doors in each compartment. However, it was said that passengers did not like having to enter and leave the coaches through only three doors, and confusion arose with the mountains of luggage normally carried in those days. Perhaps it was unfortunate that the GWR did not take the opportunity to install picture windows in the compartments instead of the traditional droplight with a quarterlight either side. In spite of the coaches' great length, passenger accommodation was not as generous as might have been expected — third-class compartments were only 5 ft 6 in between partitions, although this was standard for the time, the three vestibules using up space that might otherwise have been used for passengers.

Initially the 'Dreadnought' dining cars were marshalled in a new Paddington-Penzance express which ran non-stop between Paddington and Plymouth via Bristol, at this time the longest scheduled non-stop run in the world. This service commenced running in July 1904 for the summer period using corridor clerestory coaches plus a 'Dreadnought' diner. In the summer of 1905 the train was equipped throughout with 'Dreadnought' coaches and became the 'Cornish Riviera Express', seven coaches being the normal load. 'Dreadnought' coaches remained on the 'Cornish Riviera Express' until 1914 when they were replaced by 70 ft 'toplight' coaches.

What turned out to be the last clerestory coaches built by the GWR appeared in October 1904. They were non-gangwayed all thirds, 58 ft long, with ten compartments, and, although ordered immediately after the 'Dreadnoughts', they appeared whilst construction of the 'Dreadnoughts' was in progress.

the North to West route, or north of Wolverhampton on the Paddington-Birkenhead route, although they could use the ex-Oxford, Worcester and Wolverhampton line. In practice these restrictions were not all that onerous as there were not many 'Dreadnoughts' but, nevertheless, if a line was blocked for any reason, these lengthy vehicles could not always use alternative routes, particularly in South Wales, and their use there was not common.

When more 70 ft coaches were ordered at the time the 'Dreadnoughts' were entering service, the new vehicles were confined to a width of 9 ft, thus giving them a much wider route availability. They could reach Birkenhead, for example, and were even permitted over some of the Cambrian Railways lines. A number of them spent their entire lives on the South Wales route.

The particular feature that distinguished these coaches was the doors, one to every compartment, but, instead of following the curved contour of the coach side, they were flat. The resulting appearance gave these coaches their nickname of 'Concertina' but otherwise they had the high elliptical roof of the 'Dreadnoughts' and non-opening toplights above the main windows. The dining cars had opening toplights, similar to the 'Dreadnought' diners, and all were electrically lit. Almost the whole range of main line coaches were built in the 'Concertina' style, including some slip coaches, the first 70 ft slips, and incidentally, the first 70 ft non-gangwayed coaches.

One interesting feature of GWR coach building policy dating from the 1880s was that the building of all first-class coaches almost ceased, except for special services and suburban types. The GWR had built a large number of 6-wheel first in the 1870s and thereafter the only short

A Birmingham '2 hour' express near Ruislip hauled by a 'County' class 4–4–0. The train consists of a matching set of seven Dreadnoughts in the single colour livery. Because of their width, Dreadnoughts were not allowed north of Wolverhampton.

Collection R. S. Carpenter

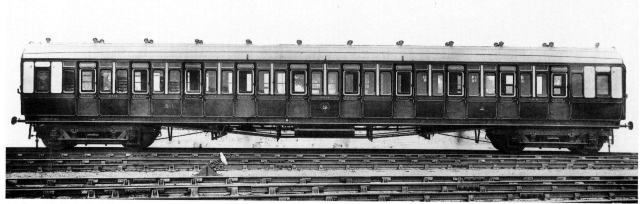

A 'concertina' all third. Note there has been a reversion to gas lighting. Diagram C27 being 70 ft long and only (!) 9 ft wide, they had a wider route availability than the Dreadnoughts.

British Railways

all-firsts were built for the London Metropolitan line services, and the first 8-wheel all-first was one of the coaches for the first corridor train. A few clerestory firsts were built, but there were no all-first, or brake first 'Dreadnought' or 'Concertina' coaches. This policy lasted until the 1930s. In practice a number of all firsts built for special services became available for general use when the special services were withdrawn and these no doubt proved an adequate supply.

The final development in coaching stock design within the period under discussion came in 1907 during the construction of Lot 1131, which consisted of 70 ft dining cars. It was decided to abandon flat recessed doors and instead make them follow the profile of the coach sides.

An empty coaching stock train outside Paddington. The coach next to the engine is a concertina slip — the first 70 ft slip coach built. On the right is a suburban train in the 1908 livery. In the background the bridge is being rebuilt and the 'Red Lion' appears by the chimney of the tank engine.

A. C. Roberts

These coaches again had the fixed toplights above all windows, except in the dining saloons which had the hinged ones, and in the absence of other distinguishing features they simply became known as 'Toplights'. Important because they were the first modern design of coach to be put into quantity production by the GWR, they were built from 1907 until 1922 and practically all types of bogie coach were built in this style, both gangwayed and non-gangwayed types, in 56ft, 57 ft and 70 ft lengths.

'Toplights', which were only 56 and 57 ft long, had a wide route availability over most of the GWR system and were accepted by most other railways. Eventually there were even shorter examples for the London City services, with the traditional sub-standard accommodation. The 70 ft long vehicles had a similar route availability to the 'Concertinas'.

'Toplight' coaches had eventful careers and underwent a certain amount of development, inevitable during such a long production run, so a short review of their design

features would be appropriate here even though many of the changes took place after 1910. They could almost always be recognised in later years, even if they had lost their toplights, by their turn-under ends and bolection mouldings round the fixed window glass. There were a couple of intermediate designs between clerestory and 'Toplight' coaches. These had very similar panelling to the earliest 'Toplight' designs but could usually be identified because they had wooden bodies with wooden mouldings but they never had toplights, or provision for them, having eaves panels instead. There were other features as well, such as the guard's 'wings' on one 70 ft brake tri-composite design, which was the only high elliptical roofed coach design to have this feature. There was also a 70 ft slab-sided sleeping car design that ran on 6-wheel bogies.

'Toplight' coaches are classified by reference to their underframes, the bodyside panelling and by their toplights. The first had underframes similar to the 'Dreadnoughts' and 'Concertinas' with round section adjustable queen-

Dining in first class style — the interior of one of the 'concertina' or early toplight period dining cars. Some of the dining cars built during the early 'toplight' period had this rather impracticable arrangement whereby the main window by each table was a droplight. Strictly speaking, these vehicles were not toplights (as they did not have them) and as their doors were not recessed they were not 'concertinas'! Notice the elaborate electric lights and the fan above the door. The furniture was in mahogany but one wonders how well they stood up to daily use. This picture was taken at Fishguard in September 1909 and is entitled 'The Boat Train G.W.R.'

BBC Hulton Picture Library

One of the 1910/1 all first class Cunard specials for the Paddington-Fishguard route. This particular set in the 1908 brown livery had the Stone's 'brake vehicle' system of lighting, evidenced by the apparatus on the end of the roof of the first coach. The locomotive is 'Star' class No. 4024, photographed in April 1911.

British Railways

posts and truss rods of flat bar stock, consequently being known as 'Bars 1' coaches. The degree of tension imparted by the truss could be altered by adjusting large nuts on the ends of the queenposts. Other recognition points of 'Bars 1' coaches were the body panelling, which was of wood with the usual mouldings, all window height panels having eaves panels above them, and on corridor coaches, the 'Bars 1' stock had two toplights above the end corridor longlights.

'Bars 2' coaches were the next development and the changes were quite subtle. They had the same underframe as 'Bars 1' coaches, but the body panelling was different. There were no eaves panels and any window height panels were extended up to the roof. Generally, 'Bars 2' corridor coaches had only one toplight above the end corridor longlight but there were some exceptions to this rule.

The third generation of 'Toplights' had different underframes and on these the queenposts were of heavy angle section and the truss rods were of circular section. The truss rods were in four separate parts, the two diagonals between the queenposts and the underframe, and the horizontal length connecting the queenposts. The last was duplicated, so that each truss had a total of four rods. Not surprisingly, these coaches are known as 'Multibar'. Adjustment of the truss was by nuts on the rods at each queenpost. The bodies of these coaches were the same as the 'Bars 2' stock initially, but from the beginning of 1913 steel panelling became the norm.

Finally the underframe was altered yet again, the queenposts and the truss rods being made of steel angle. As a result the truss was no longer adjustable, but this became standard practice thereafter. For some reason these coaches are often referred to inaccurately as 'Multibar'.

Apart from the initial batch of 70 ft dining cars, most of the 'Toplight' coaches built before 1910 were 56 or 57 ft long and gangwayed. These were followed by a one-off 70 ft brake third that had only three third class compartments and luggage space of no less than 40 ft.

This in turn was followed by some 70 ft gangwayed all firsts, including, most unusually for the GWR, some brake firsts, these coaches being intended for Paddington-Fishguard boat trains. Further 57 and 70 ft coaches were built, and when war came in 1914 most of the 56 and 57 ft coaches were sold to the War Department for use in ambulance trains.

When the war was over the GWR repurchased the survivors from the War Department and reinstated them. Many had suffered damage and all had been altered so consequently the reinstated coaches were not all to their original state. Some were given steel panelled bodies on 'Bars 1' underframes, some were rebuilt to passenger brake vans, and there were even some four-wheeled vans for milk trains apparently built from parts left over from pharmacy cars!

Before concluding this review of passenger stock development in the first ten years of the twentieth century, it is perhaps worthwhile examining the livery of carriages, there being a number of changes during the period. Traditionally the Great Western is thought of as the company with chocolate and cream coaches, but this was not always so. At the turn of the century GWR coaches were painted in what was arguably its finest livery. The coach sides were chocolate brown below the waist i.e. plain, not milk, and pale cream above, this colour quite possibly having been produced by white paint being covered with several coats of nominally clear varnish. The ends of the coach were brown, the underframe black and the roof white, often with brown below the lower rain-strip. The mouldings on the coach sides were black, lined with cream, black and gold. There is some debate as to whether the mouldings below the waist were lined in brown or black.

In 1903 a rake of coaches was painted in brown only but otherwise the livery continued, with some experimentation over the company's insignia, until 1908, when the colour was changed to overall lined brown for the coach body sides and unlined brown for the coach ends. The

'Saint' class 4–6–0 No. 2984 *Guy Mannering* (originally 4–4–2 No. 184) with a down express passing Old Oak Common East signal box. The leading four coaches are 57 ft 'toplights'. Then comes a horse-box followed by a mixture of at least seven clerestory and toplight coaches. Marshalling a light four-wheel vehicle in the middle of the train like this was frowned upon for safety reasons, but presumably this train was to be divided *en route* – possibly at Reading.
                                                                                                          Cty. R. C. Riley

passing of the brown and cream was lamented by the *Railway Magazine* which complained in October 1908 that the GWR had changed out of all recognition since 1890!

In 1912 the GWR changed the colour of its coaches again, this time to crimson lake, rather like the Midland or the South Eastern & Chatham Railways. Since a main line coach was normally only repainted every five years or so, some coaches would never have received the brown livery. With the Great War following in 1914, it is also probable that some coaches did not receive the crimson lake livery for many years after its introduction.

From the foregoing it will be seen that in six years the GWR had moved from the Victorian era of coaching stock design into the modern age. In the three following years modern methods of coach construction were adopted, putting the company ahead of other companies, most of which remained wedded to the all-wooden bodied coach.

NON PASSENGER COACHING STOCK

During the first decade of the present century, not only did passenger stock undergo a transformation but also that poorly defined group of vehicles known as 'non-passenger coaching stock' underwent similar changes. There is no precise definition of what constitutes 'non-passenger coaching stock' and practice on the GWR changed from time to time. Basically, however, this group of vehicles consisted of rolling stock which, whilst not carrying fare-paying passengers, was nevertheless intended to be regularly conveyed by passenger train at normal speeds. Consequently, these vehicles had running gear like passenger coaches although there were exceptions.

The 'non-passenger coaching stock' of the GWR can be considered in four groups although it must be emphasised that these categories are entirely unofficial

The first group to be considered are those that physically resembled passenger stock, and which were normally painted in the current passenger stock livery. Falling within this category are passenger brake vans, parcels vans, mail vans, newspaper vans and, strictly speaking, kitchen cars, although as the GWR did not have any until the 1920s they fall outside our survey.

As might be expected, the history of this group mirrored that of the contemporary coaching stock very closely. For many years until 1904, passenger brake vans, newspaper and parcels vans were normally 'low roofed' – i.e. similar to clerestory roofed coaches, but without the clerestory itself. On the other hand, mail vans, including those parcels vans used for conveying the Royal Mail, normally had clerestory roofs, more expensive than a plain roof, but no doubt considered justified on Post Office vehicles because of the staff working in them.

In addition, Post Office and newspaper vans normally had wider than standard gangway connectors so that mail bags could be easily passed through them. The connectors were also offset to one side of the vehicle, which prevented them being coupled to normal passenger corridor coaches.

The last short four-wheeled passenger brake vans were built in 1900 and henceforth gangways became the norm for all new construction of passenger brake vans and newspaper vans.

In 1901 Churchward's dynamometer car was built as one of the few vehicles with a 'royal clerestory' roof, i.e. one that sloped down to the main roof at the ends. Built with observation ends, side lookouts and an internal arrangement of two saloons, the vehicle was used for the controlled road-testing of motive power and was important in the formulation of the 'standard' range of locomotives.

The year 1903 saw the construction of four postal brake vans which had clerestory roofs, a wide, offset gangway at one end with a standard, central gangway at the other. They were built as mirror pairs, so that they could run as the leading and trailing vehicles of a train,

The GWR 40 ft low roof passenger brake van (Diagram K15). Built with style variations between 1882 and 1904, the very earliest were 10 ft wide and ran on the broad gauge. There was a central guard's compartment with luggage compartments either side. This is a late example with gangway; most did not boast this feature. It is possible that three of the coaches on the *City of Truro*'s famous run were like this.

Collection John Lewis

although they are not recorded as having done so. The GWR was rather fond of building gangwayed coaches 'left' and 'right handed' so that the corridor would run all the way along one side of a train and the carriage working books often specified which way a brake third should run. Should a coach be marshalled so that passenger accommodation was next to the locomotive, the leading compartments were normally locked out of use.

It is worth remembering that when, on 9th May 1904, *City of Truro* made its epic run from Plymouth to Bristol, the train consisted of two mail vans and three passenger brake vans, probably all 40 ft long vehicles. Therefore the speed record was held by an all non-passenger coaching stock train of old design.

Also in 1904, but just too late for the 9th May, the GWR introduced four 68 ft stowage vans for the ocean mails traffic from Plymouth. Two had guard's compartments, two were without, and the vans were built to the same body profile as the newly introduced 'Dreadnoughts'. Having high elliptical roofs and a width of 9 ft 6¾ ins, they were the first non-passenger coaching stock vehicles of modern outline. These four were followed in January 1905 by one similar which was unique on the GWR because it was a slip coach. This vehicle, conveying mail for the Midlands, Wales and the North, was detached from the ocean mail train at Bristol whilst the main train continued non-stop to London. This operation seems to have continued until about 1911, by which time, presumably, the ocean mails trains had been diverted to the Lavington route.

Seventy feet became the standard length for special vans until the end of our period, with the last 40 ft low-roof van being constructed in December 1906. Prior to this, in 1905, six 70 ft TPO vans were built, all of which had recesses for pick-up nets, although only half the number of vehicles received the equipment. All were fitted with traductor arms for setting down mail pouches at speed and all six ran in the Great Western TPO between Paddington and Penzance.

Two further ocean mails vans were built for the Fishguard services in 1908 and in general appearance they matched the 70 ft toplight coaches built for this route. The GWR had so many of the 40 ft low-roofed passenger brake vans that only three others were built between the end of 1906 and 1914. These were 57 ft long vehicles built to replace losses in the Swindon paint shop fire of 1911.

One further vehicle in this group worth noting is No. 833, a 70 ft parcels van with guard's compartment, built in October 1908. This vehicle, of somewhat bizarre appearance, had a wooden body with substantial external wood framing, rather in the manner of the GWR's milk vans. As a parcels van it was entitled to the full passenger livery, and, certainly between the wars, it was painted in chocolate and cream. This is believed to have been the only outside-framed vehicle to be so favoured and, although the design was not repeated, it lasted in service until the 1950s.

The second category of non-passenger coaching stock were vehicles of specialist construction that did not resemble coaching stock. They were painted in a simplified livery, generally chocolate, and lettered rather like goods vehicles. The primary examples of this group were horse-boxes, carriage trucks and milk vans. During the period under review, milk trucks, often referred to by their telegraphic code of 'SIPHONS', were initially painted grey but, with the livery changes of 1904, were painted brown instead.

The transport of horses and carriages by rail goes back to the earliest years of railways. Indeed, it was at one time the practice of some to travel in their own carriage which was loaded onto a wagon for conveyance by train. It must also be remembered that at the turn of the century railways had a near monopoly of inland transport, with motor vehicles very much in their infancy, poor roads and the canals very slow. So if a horse had to be moved any distance or a road vehicle conveyed, these would normally be sent by train.

During the period from 1900 to 1910 there was very little development of any significance in horse-box or carriage truck design apart from an increase in length. Carriage trucks came in two basic types, the open ones

A troop train on the Whitland-Pembroke Dock line. The leading van is a 40 ft vehicle (Diag. K4), an earlier edition of that on page 155. Open carriage trucks and three horse-boxes have been marshalled in front of the coaches.   *Photographer unknown*

being little more than flat-topped wagons. Covered vehicles, which were as tall as the loading gauge would allow, had end loading doors with a drop flap to provide a platform over the buffers. They usually had side doors as well, so that they could be used as parcels vans if required.

At the end of our period three covered 'scenery trucks' were built. These were eight-wheeled versions of the covered carriage trucks and had the same high roof profile and end loading doors. With a length of 50 ft and outside wooden framing, they were originally intended especially for the carriage of theatrical 'flats'. They were evidently judged to be successful as the design was repeated at intervals, albeit with inside framing, until the 1950s, when the last examples were built by British Railways. These eight-wheeled covered scenery trucks received the highly appropriate telegraph code of 'MONSTER'.

From the 1870s until the 1900s milk vans had been four- and later six-wheeled covered vehicles with a roof, solid boarded ends, and sides with only about half the planks present so as to keep the milk cool in transit. These vehicles had outside framing and, apart from increases in size, the basic design had not changed.

During the 1900s experiments took place with the ventilation of siphons and as a result construction changed to normal boarding up to waist level with louvres above. These louvres continued along the whole length of the van, including the door, and vehicles of this type were built on both four- and eight-wheel underframes.

The most significant development took place in 1908 when a single 50 ft bogie milk van appeared. With louvres along the upper third of the sides and doors, it was the first of the 'SIPHON Gs' which continued in production with some modifications, into the BR period. The first of these had end doors whereas most subsequent vehicles had gangways of standard type, apart from one lot coded 'SIPHON H' which had end doors and high roofs rather like the 'MONSTERS'. It was found that the revised arrangement of louvres provided adequate ventilation for milk traffic whilst keeping the interior of the van sufficiently dry to allow them to be used for general parcels work. In the 1920s new vehicles were built with internal framing, but little else of significance changed over the years.

The third category consisted of vehicles that, during the 1900s, were regarded by the GWR as freight stock but which during the Great War were reclassified as non-passenger coaching stock and renumbered accordingly. These included open fish trucks, fish vans, some fruit vans and some special cattle vans. The choice of which design of fruit van to be included in the non-passenger coaching stock category seems somewhat arbitrary, as some of those remaining in the goods series had coach type running gear whereas conversely some of the fish vans renumbered had only 'goods stock' size wheels.

There was even a fourth category of non-passenger coaching stock painted brown from about the time of the Great War but which the GWR could not otherwise

1519, a 'Siphon C' 4-wheel milk van built in 1907. These were dual-fitted originally and had Churchward's handbrake. To extend their versatility they had end as well as side doors. *British Railways*

This gas-lit horse-box of 1907 (Diag. N10) was also dual-fitted with Churchward's handbrake. Really a very smart vehicle. *HMRS*

The photographer attracts dirty looks from commuters waiting for their London-bound train while a surprisingly evenly matched milk train of 'open siphons' goes past on the down slow line. These open siphons were of a general 6-wheel design built for churn traffic from 1889 to 1905 — with variations, of course. An 'empty' milk train like this was full — of empty churns.

British Railways

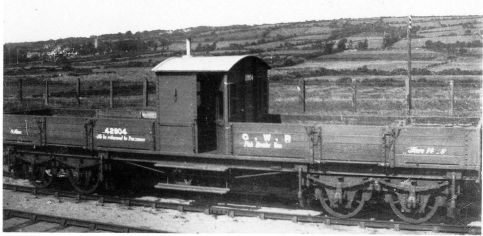

No. 42804 started life as a broad gauge fish train brake van in 1889 and is pictured here as rebuilt to standard gauge, or 'narrow gauge' as the GWR would have said. Fish in boxes was carried in the open portions of the wagon. During the Great War it was reclassified as non-passenger coaching stock and renumbered 2003. It lasted until 1926 and gave rise to any number of H. H. Bateman type jokes about 'The guard who found he had sardine sandwiches'.   *Lens of Sutton*

consider to be part of this group. These were well wagons for carrying road vehicles, machinery etc. Coded 'HYDRA', these vehicles were suitable for working in passenger trains, but not at express speeds and, although painted brown or lake initially, these wagons always retained their goods series running numbers.

So, as with passenger stock, during the ten years from 1900 to 1910, important designs of non-passenger coaching stock emerged from Swindon which set the pattern for these vehicles until the end of the GWR and beyond. The most important of these were the 'Siphon' milk vans and the 'Monster' covered scenery trucks. Both types survived the decease of their primary *raison d'être*; i.e. milk traffic in churns and scenery 'flats' conveyed on Sundays for touring theatre companies, because their value for parcels traffic had been recognised.

ARRIVAL OF A MILK TRAIN (PADDINGTON).

GOODS ROLLING STOCK

The development of goods rolling stock in the first ten years of the present century is in many ways parallel to that of passenger stock. During this period most types reached their maximum dimensions, with only minor subsequent alterations later in the 1920s and '30s to accommodate Railway Clearing House standard components. For much of the period under review, and subsequently until 1920, developments in the Carriage Works were under the direction of F. W. Marillier, an able disciple of

Churchward who transferred to Swindon in 1902 from a similar post at the Saltney Works.

In 1900, Swindon practice was, in two respects, in advance of most, if not all, other railway companies in the UK in that iron and steel underframes were standard on all new construction, and oil axleboxes were not only being fitted to all new vehicles but to any existing stock with a reasonable life expectancy. One other important development in the decade from 1900 to 1910 was the

Acton yard with contrasting old and new vans. The old ones are smaller with stout outside wooden-frames. The newer ones have metal framing to the body. Notice how tall the sheet rail is on the open wagon. The furthest open in this rake is almost certainly a hired wagon painted in GWR livery.

British Railways

standardization by the GWR of a new and efficient hand-brake for goods stock. Thus followed an extensive programme of fitting goods wagons with the automatic vacuum brake, in conjunction with the new hand brake, a move which enabled the wide expansion in 1905 of fitted goods and perishable train services.

At the turn of the century the GWR was in the process of renewing its wagon fleet, some of which dated back to the later 1860s. In fact, until recent years, the typical British goods wagon remained little changed in overall dimensions. Since that time, they were typically about 14 ft 6 in or 15 ft 6 in long and 7 ft or so wide. By 1900 they reached 16 ft and this length remained the GWR standard until the later RCH 17 ft 6 in underframe was adopted and this lasted until the end of the GWR, and into BR days.

The open wagons of 1900 exhibited a wide range of styles. The earliest dating back to 1870, or before, had one-plank wooden bodies on wooden underframes, and with an internal dimension of only 11 inches high, they did not need side doors. The railway originally had some 5,000 of these and their renewal was in no small

measure responsible for the major wagon building programme undertaken by the GWR in the 1900s.

The GWR had a wide range of open wagons which were gradually increased in height as taller vehicles were found to be more useful in traffic. Two-plank opens with side doors were the norm for most of the 1870s and their wooden underframes were the target for early renewal by the 1900s; initially there were about 4,000 of them.

Iron underframes were first experimented with during the construction of the subsequent three-plank design and from about 1881 they were standardized upon. This important step forward in wagon design was undertaken because of the increased life of iron-framed wagons, although the difficulties in obtaining suitable timber for underframes, which had to withstand the considerable shocks and stresses, was another consideration. Maintenance costs for iron underframes were greater than for wood, but repairs were less likely to be required.

From 1888 until 1902, four-plank wagons were adopted as standard and these were built in considerable quantity, finally totalling about 24,000. By 1902 an appreciable proportion of the GWR's wagon stock

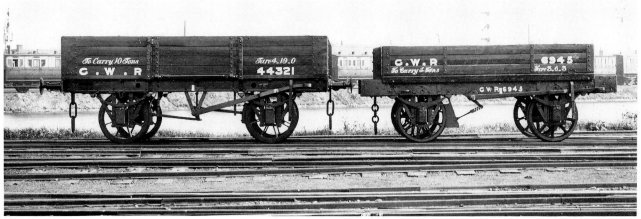

The old and the new contrasted in 1888. No. 44321 was then a new wagon of the new standard four-plank design which continued to be built until 1902. It was given OK oil axleboxes in April 1912 and sheet support in May 1915. A second lever brake was added in March 1929 and it was condemned in July 1936. 6945 (originally numbered 2002) had been built by Wright at an unknown date. It has dumb buffers — possibly one of the last of its kind in revenue service on the GWR. It had been specially repainted for this picture and was condemned in July 1888. *British Railways*

No. 67204 was built about 1897 but is shown here newly painted in its post-1904 livery. It still has grease axleboxes.
British Railways

Acton yard with a 100-wagon train behind 2—8—0 No. 2864 c.1911. This picture is a goldmine to those interested in the railway scene. It is interesting to note the extent to which loads were put into open wagons and protected by tarpaulins. In the first siding there are two of the new standard 5½ plank open wagons with tall loads, then there is a van with outside wooden framing to the body dating back to the 1880s. It still has grease axleboxes. Two wagons further on there is a long open with a tarpaulin showing how rainwater could collect and why a 'sheet rail' was an advantage. Next is a bogie bolster wagon with a very roughly sheeted load, followed by an example of the standard 16 ft van of the period. In the second siding there is an iron van which the GWR had purchased from Spillers flour millers. It is followed by three private owner coal wagons in the wordy liveries popular before the Great War. Note the contrasting grades of coal. Next comes a Great Eastern van. They looked somewhat like GWR ones, but then Holden of the GER was an ex-GWR man. Behind the GER van in the next siding is a row of meat vans *en route* either to or from Smithfield. Except for the leading van, they appear to be refrigerated vans with trapdoors in their roofs for ice. These were painted white with red lettering in this period. Note how the size of 'G' and 'W' varied to suit the wagon and avoid any ironwork.

British Railways

Hockley in February 1911 and a train of privately owned coal wagons. It was GWR policy not to provide wagons for coal traffic during this era. The leading wagon and the third wagon at least have dumb buffers — private owners (and some railway companies) were not so forward looking as the GWR. The locomotive is 0–6–0 No. 49, built as long ago as 1856 for the Oxford Worcester & Wolverhampton Railway and lasting until 1921.

H. W. Burman

consisted of these 'modern' four-plank opens and it was during their building period that oil axleboxes were introduced.

An important advantage of oil axleboxes over the earlier grease pattern was that lubrication was much more efficient, particularly when cold. A train of wagons with grease axleboxes required considerably more effort to get underway than one with oil. In addition, lubrication at speed was much improved and the incidence of 'hot boxes' lowered. The introduction of oil axleboxes and the automatic vacuum brake (discussed later) allowed the GWR to introduce its system of express goods trains from 1905 onwards.

Under Churchward, opens were increased successively to five planks, then to the equivalent of five and a half planks (by using one extra wide plank) and finally to seven planks. The latter seems to have been too much, as the GWR standardised on 5½ planks thereafter for the remainder of its existence.

In 1902 the company adopted tarpaulin rails, or sheet supports, as standard fittings for open wagons and for a while they became something of a trademark, consisting of an inverted, elongated U-shaped iron bar running the length of the wagon and pivoted at each end. When a tarpaulin was simply allowed to rest on the load, puddles

The GWR's standard unfitted open at the end of the era. It has sheet supports, self-contained buffers, Churchward's hand-brake and oil axleboxes. Unusually, this example was built by the Gloucester Railway Carriage & Wagon Co. as Swindon was over-loaded.

GRC & W Co.

could form and the water would seep through any pinholes in the sheet and spoil the goods underneath. Slung over the sheet rail, tarpaulins formed a peaked roof to repel rainfall and snow. However, as other railway companies decided that sheet supports were not worth the capital outlay, the GWR was unwilling to put open wagons so equipped into the RCH common user pool. They even began to remove the rails from the late 1920s onwards.

It is worth mentioning at this point that it was not GWR policy at this time to provide mineral wagons for coal, etc., all open wagons being 'merchandise' as opposed to 'mineral' wagons. However, the Engineer's Department was not inhibited by the presence of sheet supports, and open wagons so equipped are known to have conveyed ballast. A sheet support was a fairly heavy item and it appears that when they were fitted to the seven-plank opens, the staff had difficulty in getting them into position; they were so high that the men had to move them whilst standing on tiptoe!

Long wheelbase open wagons were experimented with, but only one design went into production for revenue, as opposed to service stock. This was a three-plank wagon, 25 ft long, which was intended for the conveyance of sawn timber.

In common with other companies, covered goods wagons were built in much smaller numbers than open wagons on the GWR. A covered wagon had the advantage of being weatherproof and avoided the trouble of tarpaulins. However, they were initially more expensive than open wagons and, unless they were provided with a roof door, could not be unloaded by crane. At one time there had been a vogue for roof doors in covered wagons, but they were difficult to keep weathertight and by 1900 the GWR had done away with them.

The design of covered goods wagons remained remarkably static until the advent of the Churchward era when a number of high capacity types were introduced. Although not unsuccessful, these were not built in large numbers and the subsequent designs settled down once more and lasted until BR days. Prior to 1887 the standard GWR covered goods wagon was an all wooden bodied vehicle with substantial outside framing. Typically they were about 15 ft 6 in long and 6 ft 8 in high inside. The change-

No. 81537 was built in 1907/8. It had vacuum and Churchward handbrake and leaf spring buffers. It was one of a batch of 500 of these wagons. It is a 5½ plank wagon with a wide top plank — the standard new production of that period and for some while thereafter.

British Railways

The GWR, as with other railways, were 'common carriers'. This photograph, taken at Newbury, shows some of the variety of small traffic carried, with boxes of Sunlight soap and galvanized iron water tanks in evidence. Barrels like these did not contain beer, but other products, and the whole business of loading and unloading was very labour intensive.

British Railways

over from wooden underframes to iron took place between 1879 and 1881, 2,400 being built during a period when 10,000 opens were constructed.

From time to time throughout its history, the GWR experimented with, and occasionally adopted, iron or steel bodied wagons. In 1887 and 1888 they built just two covered vehicles, a cattle wagon and a goods brake van both with iron bodies. A similar bodied covered goods wagon was also constructed but, even before the prototype appeared, the design was put into quantity production. This was the famous 'iron mink', an unofficial term incidentally, 'MINK' being the telegraph code for 'covered goods wagon'.

Iron vans had the twin advantages of being both stronger and longer lasting than wooden-bodied vans, and the 'iron mink' design was copied by many railways in South Wales. A number of private companies also adopted the design — in particular Spillers & Co. for carrying flour, and some cement manufacturers — and they were used by the Railway Clearing House as a basis for gunpowder wagons. In this way the design appeared on many railways throughout the country, and a modified version was even produced by British Railways. 16 ft 'iron minks' remained in production on the GWR until 1901.

Two specialist wooden wagons were also produced during this period: a double-skinned meat van with smooth outside planking (i.e. no external framing) and a fruit van. The meat vans could be refrigerated with ice, later 'dry ice', and remained the railway's standard design for vehicles of this type. The fruit van, of approximately the same dimensions as the 'iron mink', had external framing now of iron or steel flat straps and, 'L' and 'T' sections, but the doors remained wooden framed — another GWR trademark.

No. 47777 was a van (Mica) for fresh meat, Unlike the refrigerated versions, it was painted grey. Notice it has passenger standard running gear with 3 ft 7 in Mansell wheels and Armstrong's moving vacuum cylinder (a GWR speciality). This particular example dated back to January 1892, but it was not very different to those built in the 1900s. It lasted until 1944 and is seen here in post-1904 livery.   *J. P. Richards*

This view was taken in 1914. No. 73614 was one of 200 4-plank opens and was built in 1900, whilst 45674, of the same design, dates back to another lot of 200 built in 1889. 16204 was then the latest in GWR vans complete with vacuum brakes, self-contained buffers and dual bonnet end ventilators instead of the louvred ones with sliding covers of earlier examples. The 3-plank open is quite an ancient one (pre-1888). Note the shunting truck next to the loco, a GWR speciality.   *British Railways*

A deserted scene! Note all the carts awaiting loading and the 'Iron Mink' wagon dwarfed by the Mink D 28 ft 6 in long next to it. Curiously, they were both rated at 10-ton load in due course. The picture was taken in Paddington Goods.

British Railways

Wagon ends at Paddington Goods. On the left is a covered carriage truck identifiable by its end doors and high roof. The selection of vans demonstrates the differences between the older designs with end louvre ventilators and sliding covers, and the later designs with twin end bonnet ventilators. Note the capstans for moving wagons, the weighted point lever and the wooden ramps to check rails (left) to stop ropes snagging.   *British Railways*

By 1902 the initial cost differential between iron and the equivalent wooden-bodied vans had reached about £10 in favour of the latter so the GWR reverted to the cheaper option. For the first two years the wooden vans were built to the same dimensions as the 'iron minks', i.e. 16 ft long and 7 ft high inside.

Covered goods vehicles tended to be used for loads that were bulky but of relatively low weight. With two excep-

tions, the GWR investigated vans of larger dimensions (both length and height), but without the commensurate increases in load-bearing capacity. The increase in height internally ranged from 7 ft to 8 ft, after which 7 ft 6 in was adopted as standard for the remainder of the GWR's history.

The first vehicles longer than the standard 16 ft dimension were 21 ft long with two pairs of sliding doors. Only

A Mink C (Diag. V7 Lot 546) 20 ft 10½ in long, built 1906-7, with Churchward brakegear, Churchward vacuum cylinder, leaf spring buffers, and 3-link couplings in spite of being vacuum braked. Instanter couplings would have been fitted later.   *British Railways*

Westbourne Terrace bridge between Paddington and Royal Oak about 1908. On the left the approach tracks to Paddington Goods are just visible in the background. On the extreme left there is the Red Lion . . . ! In the centre are the electrified lines of the Hammersmith and City Railway and on the right the lines into Paddington station. As this picture was taken before common user wagons, it is perhaps not surprising that there are no 'foreigners'. The wagons on the left include two Micas like 47777 on page 167, a standard 5½ plank open and a Mink C like that on page 169. The next siding has, largely concealed, an unidentified GWR van with a nearly flat roof, a Mink C, and an open with tarpaulin over the sheet support. On the next siding is a pair of 28 ft 6 in Mink Ds next to a Mink C with a 16 ft 'Iron Mink' further down the train. The nearest of the row of three goods brake vans (Toads) is an old example with an outside wooden-framed body and just above the third Toad in this line is a 4-wheel 'Crocodile' trolley wagon, and end on behind it is a covered carriage truck. In the left foreground the engineer has got hold of some merchandise wagons, one with a tarpaulin bar. Note the PW trolley with its wheel sets removed in the foreground and the structure gauge on the ground. The main line signals have lettered on them which line they apply to (not much help at night!). For the view looking the other way, see page 194.

British Railways

These are two examples of the GWR's purpose-built 'pilot vans' of the period before the Great War. No. 3 is a tender to the breakdown van No. 2 on the left-hand side of the picture and was built in June 1910 on a second-hand carriage underframe. It lasted until 1966. No. 2, the breakdown van, was built a couple of months earlier.

*L & GRP
cty. David & Charles*

six were built with this unusual feature, subsequent ones having the usual hinged doors. Five hundred were constructed between 1904 and 1907, but thereafter the only vehicles of this length were for the special traffics of fish and fruit. With a length of 28 ft 6 in, the next design also had two pairs of double doors and a load capacity of 10 tons. 126 were built in total and again fish and fruit vans were built to the same length.

The final covered goods design of the period under review was the 'Mink F', an iron van carried on eight wheels. Completed in 1904, they were 36 ft long with a capacity of 30 tons. The reason for their construction is a mystery as their cost approached almost twice that of the contemporary 28 ft 6 in vans. However, whilst these longer vehicles were in production, the GWR continued building the 16 ft version in quantity, with over 2,000 completed by 1910. Apart from minor changes to the drawgear, brakes and buffing gear, the design remained in production until 1927, when the length was increased to accommodate a 17 ft 6 in RCH underframe. With the addition of a new style flush-planked door, the revised design continued in production until BR days.

On most railways the various engineers departments made do with life-expired carriages and wagons for tool vans, mess vans etc. This was also the case on the GWR except between the late 1890s and the First World War, when the Civil Engineer's and the Signal Engineer's Departments and Henry Pooley & Co., the GWR's weighing machinery contractors, had vans specially built for them. These were mostly iron-bodied and seem to have spent much of their long lives sitting in out-of-the-way sidings. Provided the rust was kept at bay, their maintenance costs must have been very low.

The Locomotive, Carriage and Wagon Department also had their own special vans, in this case for breakdown crews. The Victorians could not bear to call a spade a spade when a euphemism was available: 'breakdown' had overtones of 'accident' so for many years these vans were called 'pilot vans'. Having vertically planked wooden bodies, they were normally accompanied by very similar vehicles with living accommodation — called 'tenders'. The breakdown vans were equipped with a wide range of tools including jacks, hammers, saws, spanners, wooden packing, etc; and the crew were expected to deal with minor derailments (e.g. of wagons in goods yards) without the use of a crane.

Special wagons, such as the fish and fruit vans built after 1900, were adaptations of the standard van design with additional ventilation and, in the case of banana vans, heating. The fish vans began to supplement and then replace some old ex-broad gauge fish trucks which were simply long open wagons fitted with coaching stock running gear.

One of the more interesting sights of the period was that of long timber, particularly tree trunks, being carried by rail. Traditionally, such loads were carried on short wagons, each having a single bolster (or timber baulk) with iron stanchions to restrain the load. This was chained tightly to the bolsters to ensure that it did not move relative to the wagon during transit. The bolsters were designed to rotate to allow the load (and the wagons) to negotiate curves. When the load was too long for a pair of wagons (about 30 ft), additional vehicles were provided to distance the bolster wagons and to act as 'runners' under the overhang at each end. Photographs exist showing no fewer than six wagons under a particularly long cargo. There were strict rules regarding the carriage of long items and loading was a skilled task. One important factor was that the intermediate wagons and the end runners *all* had to be kept clear of the load, especially on sharp bends, otherwise the ensemble would derail. Sometimes they did — usually in goods yards while negotiating tight curves and pointwork.

The Churchward regime introduced longer 8-wheel bolster wagons, 45 ft in length and capable of carrying 30 tons. These made the conveyance of long loads much simpler, although the loading rules still applied for the longest. These vehicles were coded 'MACAW B' by the GWR's telegraph section and were the direct ancestors of

axlebox technology improved and, with larger journals, 4 wheels became the norm.

Because of injuries and loss of life caused to shunters trying to fasten or release brakes that were inefficient or difficult to operate, experiments in this field were carried out around the turn of the century. This movement culminated in the regulations issued by the Board of Trade in 1911 setting out standards for wagon hand brakes. In particular the brakes were to be 'right-handed' — i.e. the

A pair of Macaw Bs built about 1908. This sort of load would have needed six or more single bolster trucks if the load had been carried a few years earlier.   *GWR Magazine*

similar bogie bolster wagons in use on BR today. In 1912 the GWR built two 70 ft bogie bolster wagons for the conveyance of rails. These were the longest of their kind and were not allowed off the GWR without permission.

Goods brake vans underwent little change in appearance during the first years of this century remaining the same size as they had been since the introduction of the design in the 1880s. However, they did get heavier — from 10-12 tons up to 25 tons — and this was achieved by adding scrap iron to 'pockets' in the underframe. From 1900 to 1902 the heavy brake vans had six wheels, but thereafter

brake lever should be towards the right-hand end of the wagon as the shunter faced it; the mechanical advantage should be such that the brake could 'be conveniently applied with one hand' and the brake should only be released from the side of the wagon from which it had been applied.

The GWR was no different to other railways in this respect and Mr. Thomas, manager of the Carriage & Wagon Department at Swindon, was granted a patent for a hand brake in 1897. Thomas's brake had a crank handle which was turned to apply the brakes via a linkage which

The GWR standard brake van built from about 1888 until BR days — with variations but still recognizable. No. 17539 in fact dates back to 1889 and was one of the first of this design. It is allocated to GWR Crewe and when the photo was taken, was in the charge of guard J. Young. This particular diagram was built from 1888 until 1901 (Diag. AA3).

Collection John Lewis

Applying the GWR wagon handbrake. This was the pre-Churchward brake on which the lever was held down by teeth in the rack — not easy to apply on a moving wagon. This photo was taken at 'GWR brake and shunting trials' at Acton, 15th June 1906.

BBC Hulton Picture Library

involved a worm wheel. It appears to have been efficient compared with the contemporary lever hand brake, but it took a relatively long time to apply or release. It also had the disadvantage that to apply the brake on one side of the wagon, the handle was turned clockwise, whilst on the other the same movement released it! In 1899 the GWR equipped some goods stock with Thomas's patent hand brake but because it was slow to apply and release, it did not comply with Board of Trade regulations. The Thomas brake was replaced by 1914 on most stock so fitted, but two of the Signal Department's iron vans kept theirs until 1938 which gives an indication of how often they visited Swindon!

After further experiments, a patent was granted in 1902 to Dean (who was then still Locomotive, Carriage and Wagon Superintendent) and Churchward jointly for another hand brake. With short brake levers and circular hand guards, this design became the standard hand brake on the GWR until the 1920s when, with some reluctance, it would appear, Morton's lever brake was adopted for most general purpose wagons.

The essential feature of the Dean-Churchward brake was a linkage that gave a considerable mechanical advantage combined with a pawl and ratchet arrangement. To apply the brake, the handle was lowered and the pawl engaged the ratchet to keep the brake 'on'. To release the brake, the handle was raised until a lever on the

The Churchward brake was much easier to apply or release than other types!   *BBC Hulton Picture Library*

hand brake shaft knocked the pawl out of the ratchet, whereupon the brake came 'off'. It was simple to use and made the shunter's task much easier, although, because it could be released from either side of the wagon, it did not comply precisely with the Board of Trade's regulations.

Churchward was also responsible for the introduction of a revised vacuum brake arrangement following an accident at Slough in 1900. This involved fitting a valve to admit air directly to the brake system in an emergency, thus stopping the train more quickly. At the same time Churchward introduced a new design of vacuum brake cylinder where the piston moved in a fixed cylinder. The previous (Armstrong) type had a moving cylinder and a fixed piston! This new automatic vacuum brake was applied, with great vigour between 1906 to 1910, to much of the wagon stock, thus allowing the expansion of the GWR's newly established express goods train services, intended to provide next day delivery running over

considerable distances non-stop at speeds of around 40 mph. For this reason, vehicles with grease axleboxes and wheelbases less than 9 ft, were prohibited from the new trains, thus excluding most private owners and wagons belonging to other railway companies. In the four years after 1906 the GWR equipped over 5,000 wagons (apart from fish, fruit and meat vans) with the automatic vacuum brake, which explains why other companies' express goods trains had the 'fitted head' made up largely of GWR wagons.

Thus, during the first decade of this century, the GWR introduced many of the wagon designs which remained standard throughout the remainder of the company's history and which even influenced some British Railways designs. It also improved safety by the introduction of new and efficient brakes and established a network of express goods train services which gave overnight transit of goods between most important centres on the railway.

British Railways

Motor bus adapted for publicising the company's facilities, seen near Paddington. The bus was used for the purpose in a number of locations including Scotland.

British Railways

CHAPTER SEVEN

OTHER DEVELOPMENTS

JOHN NORRIS

THE story of achievement has dealt so far with the major developments, but many other works were undertaken, large and small, the length and breadth of the system. Year after year the company sought and obtained powers for the compulsory purchase of land, often in quite small parcels, needed for new bridges, widening schemes, or simply for the enlargement of local goods yards. Much of the quadrupling which remains a familiar feature today, had already been undertaken, notably that between Paddington and Didcot. At the end of 1899 there were 68 route-miles of four-line track, and 10 miles with five or more lines. At the end of 1910 the figures were 91 and 30 respectively, the increases being mainly in the Birmingham area and in South Wales, but the improved approaches to several important stations will also have made their contribution, while the work of

quadrupling the tunnel at the west end of Newport station was nearing completion. Although the approaches to Paddington have been simplified in recent years, the scene, and in particular the substantial road bridges over the several running lines, remains very much as it became during the period of our review.

In the West Country the century began with a considerable amount of single track, even on the main lines, and it was not until 1905, with the doubling of the tunnels at Dawlish, that there was a double-line throughout from Paddington to Plymouth. West of Plymouth, much work was undertaken with the replacement of the Brunel timber viaducts, all of which were single-line; in the case of the section between Saltash and St. Germans, some three miles of completely new line were built to avoid rebuilding the viaducts on the original line which ran very

'Duke' class 4—4—0 locomotive piloting two 0—6—0STs on a train of empty ballast wagons near Rattery Siding.

L & GRP, cty. David & Charles

Preparatory work at a Brunel viaduct for the replacement of the timber staging by iron girders.

British Railways

New viaduct under construction on the diversion between Saltash and St. German's in Cornwall. *British Railways*

Left: Parson Tunnel near Dawlish before widening for double track. The width of the tunnel for a single line on the broad gauge can clearly be seen. *Right:* Phillot Tunnel near Dawlish, freshly reconstructed for double track. *British Railways*

Henbury station between Stoke Gifford and Avonmouth.   *British Railways*

much nearer to the River Lynher, crossing various creeks as it did so. Elsewhere on the system, widening for double track took place on such diverse sections as those between Ruabon and Llangollen, Torquay and Paignton, and Adderbury and Kings Sutton.

Other new lines were constructed, and perhaps the one having the greatest economic significance was that to serve the expanding port of Avonmouth, where the original dock had been opened in 1877. It was served by both the GWR and the MR over their joint line via Clifton. Additional rail access had been provided by the GWR in 1900 with a line from Pilning. This was intended to improve the flow of traffic between South Wales and Avonmouth, making use of the Severn Tunnel, even though such traffic had to reverse at Pilning as the junction there faced east.

The opening of the Royal Edward Dock by King Edward VII on 9th July 1908 introduced a completely new dimension as far as the traffic demands of the port on the railways were concerned. The GWR met the situation by constructing a new line, 6¾ miles in length, which left the Pilning section at Holesmouth Junction, and joined the South Wales & Bristol Direct Railway at Stoke Gifford. This was brought into use on 9th May 1910, enabling traffic to pass directly between Avonmouth and stations reached by way of Swindon, as well as those by way of Yate and Gloucester.

Avonmouth was traditionally associated with the West Indian trade, having a specialised traffic in bananas for which the GWR would operate as required trains of special steam-heated vans. Passenger traffic through the port sometimes justified a special train to or from Paddington, and this would normally run via Stoke Gifford. On other occasions the passengers could be accommodated in coaches added to the regular trains between Paddington and Bristol, and worked specially between Temple Meads and Avonmouth Dock station. For such workings, special carriage boards were introduced bearing the words *Imperial Direct West India Mail Service, Jamaica via Avonmouth.*

Not so very far from Avonmouth the line from Camerton to Limpley Stoke, nearly eight miles, was completed in May 1910, its principal purpose being to provide an outlet for Dunkerton Colliery in the Somersetshire coalfield. It had been laid very largely on the alignment of the disused Somersetshire Coal Canal. Further west, in Cornwall, a line had been opened in 1903 to link Perranporth with the main line to Penzance at Chacewater west of Truro, and at the beginning of 1905 an extension had been opened to Shepherds on the branch from Newquay to Treamble, part of the former Cornwall Minerals Railway. This development entailed the construction of some twelve miles of new line, and the upgrading for passenger trains of five miles of the Treamble branch. The completed work gave Newquay direct access to Truro but as an outlet for extended mineral workings between Perranporth and Newquay, it probably proved something of a disappointment.

Nearer London the year 1907 saw the completion of a branch of about two miles to Uxbridge (High Street) from the GW & GC joint line near Denham. Uxbridge was already served by the much older branch from West Drayton to its station at Vine Street, but ideas for a connection between the two never came to fruition. In the following year the Coley branch at Reading was brought into use. This was about 1¾ miles in length, leaving the Newbury line at Southcote Junction where the Basingstoke line also diverged, and was built purely to serve a new central goods station for the town.

The increased traffic generated by so many of the improvements led to demands for other developments. Many passenger stations were quite inadequate to deal with the traffic which they were called upon to handle, even if it were only a case that the platforms had often been built to accommodate much shorter trains than were now being run. New or enlarged goods stations were needed if the growing volume of traffic were to be handled expeditiously, while modern installations were needed to service the expanding locomotive fleet.

New central goods station at Reading at the terminus of the Coley branch, seen soon after its opening in 1908.

British Railways

Rebuilding work in progress at Exeter (St. David's) c.1910.

British Railways

Sometimes stations or locomotive depots were built on new sites to enable the old ones to be used for other purposes. Such was the case at Pontypool Road where a new and much enlarged passenger station was completed in 1909, replacing the previous station a little to the south, the site of which was used to improve the flow of goods traffic. Much as a larger locomotive depot was wanted to serve Paddington, the building of the new depot at Old Oak Common during the period was rendered more urgent by the need to use the site of the depot at Westbourne Park in connection with improvements to the approaches to Paddington. Similar thinking will have led to the decision to build a new locomotive depot for Birmingham at Tyseley, to replace that at Bordesley.

At Wolverhampton a new locomotive depot was built at Oxley, essentially for goods workings, to relieve the pressure at the Stafford Road depot which was largely given over to passenger duties. The situation in Bristol was very much the same with a new depot at St. Phillip's Marsh to relieve that at Bath Road. Elsewhere new depots were brought into use or planned at Leamington, Stratford-on-Avon, Carmarthen, Stourbridge Junction, Severn Tunnel Junction and Newport, among other places.

The depot at Newport was part of a much larger scheme there which did not get fully under way until after the end of our period; it included new goods offices and the complete rebuilding of the passenger station at High Street. Extensive alterations and improvements were carried out at Exeter (St. David's) around the end of the period.

For goods traffic, large new depots were constructed at Bristol (Canon's Marsh) and at South Lambeth. The

Pontypool Road. *Above:* the new station. *Below:* the old station.   *British Railways*

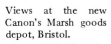

Views at the new Canon's Marsh goods depot, Bristol.
GWR Magazine

The scene at Slough
after the crash in 1900.
*Collection
E. Mountford*

latter is of interest in that it lay off GWR territory, and could be reached only by the West London and West London Extension Railways, and a section of the South Eastern & Chatham Railway. When the first part of the depot was brought into use in 1910, it was hailed as a major benefit to the distribution of milk in South London, which had previously been carted from Paddington. Also dating from the period was the large office block for goods traffic in Bishop's Bridge Road, Paddington.*

The GWR had a proud record for safety. This was due in no small measure to the adoption of automatic train control, whereby audible indications were given in the cab of an engine as to the state of distant signals, and if an adverse warning were ignored by the crew, automatic application of the brakes would follow. Precisely what prompted the GWR to carry out the necessary experiments is far from clear, although the death of five persons in a collision at Slough in 1900 may have caused the company to give serious thought to the way in which similar accidents might be prevented in the future. On this occasion, with perfect visibility on a summer afternoon, an express from Paddington ran into the back of a train for Windsor which was standing at the platform in Slough station. From the evidence given at the subsequent inquiry, it was clear that the express had run past several signals at danger before the impact. Some six months before this accident, another collision had occurred at Slough in thick fog, but this happily was not attended with fatal results.

An experimental system of audible signals on the Henley-on-Thames branch, then double line, became fully operational on 1st January 1906. The system required the installation of a ramp between the rails near each distant signal, and this depressed a shoe fitted on the

underside of locomotives employed on the branch. When the distant signal had been lowered, an electrical circuit was completed through the ramp and the shoe, activating a bell in the cab. If the signal were at danger, the electricity supply to the ramp was switched off and the depression of the shoe caused a whistle to be blown in the cab instead. In both cases the driver had to take action to stop the audible signal, while he was, of course, alerted by the whistle as to the need to apply the brakes. Shortly afterwards some experiments commenced on the main line when it became possible to evaluate the results with an engine travelling at a much greater speed.

The trials on the Henley branch were so successful that on 1st December 1906 they were extended to the Fairford branch. The purpose of these further experiments was twofold; firstly there was the need to overcome the problem arising on a single line as a result of trains passing over a ramp in both directions, while secondly it was necessary to study the effects of a decision to remove the arms of all distant signals on the branch, and to rely entirely on the audible signals. It had thus to be arranged that only locomotives equipped with audible signals were allowed on the branch, and an additional ramp was laid at the locomotive sheds at both Oxford and Fairford so that the signals might be tested before a locomotive set out.

By the end of 1908 ramps had been installed at the distant signals on all four lines between Slough and Reading, and a sufficient number of engines had been fitted with audible signals, so that the system was already making a valuable contribution to train operation and safety. Two years later its use had been extended through to Paddington.

An important development took place in September 1909 with the commencement of practical tests of the

*Recently demolished.

automatic application of the brakes following an adverse audible signal. The line chosen for this stage of the experiments was the branch from Newbury to Lambourn. There was, however, one modification from the system on the Fairford branch in that, although distant signals were removed, they were treated by the replacement ramps as if they were fixed signals and, hence, permanently at danger. Accordingly, drivers always received the adverse audible signal in the cab, which would be followed by the automatic application of the brakes.

In 1910 the audible cab-signalling apparatus was shown at the Brussels Universal Exhibiton, and the GWR received an Honours Diploma for its achievement.

No further steps appear to have been taken to dispense with the arms of distant signals which were clearly of great assistance to the drivers of fast trains, particularly when the signals were so sited as to be seen from a considerable distance ahead. However, they were never restored on the line to Fairford, which remained without distant signals to the end of its days.

With the intervention of the war years and an investigation into automatic train control by a government departmental committee, no extension of the system took place until 1929, when it was brought into use from Reading to Swindon and Oxford, and from Paddington to High Wycombe. This extension was combined with the widespread fitting of audible signals and the automatic braking device to locomotives. By the autumn of 1931 the system was in use through to Plymouth, both via Bristol and via Westbury, from Westbury to both Weymouth and Salisbury, on the main line through to Swansea, and on all main lines east of, and including, the route from Wolverhampton through Worcester and Hereford to Newport, giving a total distance under control of 2,130 track miles. By early 1938 a further 710 track miles had been covered, including the remainder of the lines through to Penzance, Fishguard and Chester, as well as the Shrewsbury & Hereford Joint Line, and some 2,900 locomotives had been equipped.

The GWR had a well-established shipping service from Weymouth to the Channel Islands at the beginning of the century, a service which continues to this day. Changes to its services to Southern Ireland have been described already, but mention still needs to be made of its attempts to establish services to the French ports of Brest and Nantes.

Great Western interest in such services appears to have begun with the chartering of one of its vessels, normally employed on the run to the Channel Islands, by fruit growers in Britanny for the export of their produce to the United Kingdom through Brest and Plymouth. First reports of the charters occurred in 1907. Passengers were certainly being carried in the summer of that year, even though the service was not on a regular basis. In the October of that year about 150 passengers paid the fare of one guinea for a long day-excursion from Paddington to Brest via Plymouth, the S.S. *Roebuck* being used for the sea passage.

At an early date it was realised that the company was acting outside its powers in operating the service to Brest, and the result was an application to parliament in the session of 1908-9 for leave to bring in a bill to regularise the situation. This duly received the royal assent on 16th August 1909, and authorised the company to operate steamboat services between Weymouth and Plymouth on the one hand, and on the other hand, ports in the Channel Islands, Cherbourg, and ports on the French coast between St. Malo and Nantes (inclusive). It was a requirement that the vessels used should be registered at a British port, except in the case of temporary chartering.

While the sailings to Brest had continued despite the doubts as to their legality, the GWR awaited the outcome of the proceedings in parliament before commencing a weekly service between Weymouth and Nantes. Because of the volume of Channel Islands traffic at Weymouth, the Nantes sailings were transferred to Plymouth and increased to bi-weekly for the summer season of 1910. For the service to Brest, and in time for the same season, the GWR purchased the S.S. *Chelmsford* from the GER, renaming it *Bretonne*.

Towards the end of the summer season of 1911 there were reports of the impending abandonment of both services. Unhappily, as far as Nantes was concerned, the reports proved to be true. The company persevered with its sailings to Brest for another two years before withdrawing that service as well. At the general meeting in February 1914 the chairman told shareholders that it was not a satisfactory service, and that there was no chance of being able to resume it, even for the summer months, with the prospect of making it a paying proposition.

In the summer of 1900 a remarkable range of through passenger services was already in existence, some of them probably seasonal. Even though at the time the Cambrian Railways were more closely associated with the LNWR than with the GWR, there were through coaches between Paddington and Aberystwyth via Shrewsbury and Welshpool, while in the West Country the branches to Falmouth, Fowey, Ilfracombe, Minehead and Newquay were similarly served to and from Paddington. More surprisingly, however, there was a daily through coach from Paddington to Brecon, outward via Gloucester to Hereford, but via Worcester on the return. There were also through coaches in each direction between Manchester and both Paddington and Worcester, via Market Drayton and Wellington, and between Paddington and Southampton, outward via Reading and Basingstoke, but returning via Newbury.

Several cross-country services were well-established, including those on the West-to-North route through Hereford, between Cardiff and Portsmouth, between Birkenhead and Bournemouth, and between Birmingham and Cardiff via Hereford. Although experiments had been made with through coaches between the GWR and resorts on the south-east coast as far back as 1864, none are shown in 1900, while through services to and from the GCR via Banbury had yet to be introduced.

By 1910, however, the association with the GCR had had a considerable impact on the GWR, and the company was feeling the benefit from its foresight in assisting the GCR financially over the construction of the line between Woodford and Banbury. Quite apart from the large amount of goods traffic exchanged at Banbury, there

Bewdley c.1909, with 70 ft steam railmotor No. 91 in brown livery. The LNWR through coach is at the rear of a Birmingham-bound train from Wooferton Junction, on the Shrewsbury and Hereford GWR/LNWR Joint line, and has reached Bewdley over the Wyre Forest line. The roofboard reads 'Through Carriage Between Birmingham and Wooferton via Smethwick'.   *Lens of Sutton*

were through passenger workings between the GCR and places such as Bristol, Bournemouth and Southampton. In some instances the GCR coaches were worked to and from Southampton via Didcot and Newbury.

The value of through services with the GCR led the GWR to construct two short pieces of line by which a new passenger train could be operated between South Wales and places in the north-east of the country. Such a train could have been worked to and from Banbury on the GWR by way of the Severn Tunnel, Didcot and Oxford, but instead the company took advantage of the much shorter route offered by what was known as its Banbury & Cheltenham Direct Railway. In reality this consisted of two separate branches from Chipping Norton Junction (renamed Kingham in 1909), situated between Oxford and Worcester, but these were now connected by a fly-over spanning the Worcester line, which at least gave the railway the directness implied in its title. Additionally, a new connection known as the Hatherley Loop was built at Cheltenham to enable trains on the Banbury line to run to and from the direction of Gloucester without reversing.

The new train was introduced on 1st May 1906. Including a restaurant car, it was made up of GW and GC coaching stock on alternate days. Initially it ran between Cardiff and Newcastle, but was later extended to serve Barry and Swansea, and with a portion for Hull added, it became known familiarly as the 'Ports-to-Ports Express'. In order that Cheltenham might be adequately served, Leckhampton station on the Banbury line was rebuilt and renamed 'Cheltenham South & Leckhampton'.

A further innovation, with a view to improving travel between South Wales and East Anglia, was made on 10th

July 1908. This took the form of a through train between Cardiff and Lowestoft and Yarmouth, thus saving passengers the need to cross London. As between Cardiff and Gloucester it was attached to the 'Ports-to-Ports' train, but otherwise it ran independently on the GWR, calling at Cheltenham (Malvern Road) and Stratford to Leamington where it was handed over to the LNWR. It then continued to Peterborough, and the GER then took charge. The service operated for the duration of the summer timetables of 1908 and 1909, but was not revived in 1910. A factor contributing to its lack of success may well have been the slow schedules which applied on the GER. These were in marked contrast to those on the LNWR, which provided for one stop only between Leamington and Peterborough — at Wansford eastbound, and at Rugby westbound. The train consisted of two coaches only, supplied by the GWR and the GER on alternate days.

To cater for the service between South Wales and East Anglia, a new connection was put in between the GWR and LNWR at the east end of Leamington (GWR) station. While this was probably little used for other passenger traffic, it became a valuable link around the time of the 1914 war, when iron ore was worked that way from Northamptonshire to South Wales.

Another through service worthy of mention was introduced in 1910 between Manchester and Bournemouth. This ran via Crewe, Market Drayton and Wellington. South of Wellington, operation took various forms over the years, sometimes as an independent train, sometimes attached to the services to and from Birkenhead. The variations in operation included non-stop running in both directions between Crewe and Wolverhampton. The introduction of this service pre-dates that of the better-known 'Pines Express' over the Somerset & Dorset route.

The first ten years of the century also saw a remarkable increase in slip-coach working, both in the number of services and in the number of places at which it occurred. The complexities of the operation had increased out of all recognition since its introduction in 1858, not least of all with the techniques of sealing the vacuum brake pipes, and, nearer to our time, the sealing of the pipes for steam heating. To assist guards in charge of slip vehicles, a marker board would sometimes be erected up to half-a-mile from the point at which the vehicles were to be brought to a stand, and the board was then the guide to the completion of the disconnection procedure.

Midway through 1910, timetables show slip-working in the down direction at some 25 locations, and 8 in the up, these figures represent a doubling of the total ten years before. Two locations (Taplow and Swindon), which appeared in 1900, had dropped out by 1910, while Southall is known to have been added and deleted within the ten years. The most prolific place to witness the working would have been Reading, where as many as a dozen trains in the up direction slipped a portion during the course of a normal weekday.

For many years spanning our period, a down evening express from Paddington slipped a portion at Tilehurst, and it was then worked forward to serve the local stations as far as Cholsey & Moulsford, so that business travellers returning home from London were saved time, and presumably the need to change trains at Reading as well. Arrangements of a similar nature were made at Lapworth and at Knowle, whereby slip-coaches from Paddington were worked forward to serve suburban stations towards Birmingham. In the same area slip-working for passengers from Birmingham was of regular occurrence at both Hatton and Warwick; in the case of the slips at Hatton, the coaches were normally for Stratford-on-Avon. Coaches were sometimes added to trains at Birmingham to be slipped at Wellington (Salop), while in the days before the opening of the direct line through Bicester, Oxford also received passengers once a day from the Birmingham direction by slip-coach.

One problem created by the slip-coach was that it was often impossible to provide a return service comparable in speed. This may be exemplified by the slip for Cheltenham, introduced at Chipping Norton Junction on 1st May 1906 from the 1.40 p.m. down Worcester express. By this service a passenger could reach Cheltenham from Paddington in 2½ hours, a saving of half-an-hour or more compared with the best time available via Swindon and Gloucester. In the reverse direction the coaches were worked by the same route, but with the shunting required at Chipping Norton Junction, no significant saving was achieved compared with the journey time via Swindon.

A more extreme example arose at Carmarthen Junction when the day boat train to Fishguard commenced to slip a portion for Aberystwyth. Stopping only at Carmarthen, Pencader and Lampeter, it provided the unusual spectacle of an express passenger train on the Manchester & Milford line, and it brought Aberystwyth within seven hours of

One of the original railmotors for the service in the Stroud Valley. *Collection R. C. Riley*

Paddington. No attempt was made to provide a fast service in the opposite direction and the journey times ranged from about 1½ to 2½ hours longer.

Not all the unusual and interesting through coaches were slip-workings. By the end of our period the 1.40 p.m. from Paddington had coaches for Shrewsbury which went forward from Worcester by different routes, the one being via the Severn Valley, and the other via Hereford to provide a service without change of carriage from Paddington to places such as Leominster and Ludlow. The coaches returned by the same route, meeting at Worcester on the 2.00 p.m. express, non-stop to Paddington.

By this time the through coaches to Brecon and Fowey of 1900 had ceased but Kingsbridge had joined the West Country branches having a through coach to and from Paddington.

The GWR was a leading exponent of the use of steam rail-motors. These were purpose-built coaches, varying in length and in their detailed fittings, but each embodying a small steam engine which could be driven from either end of the vehicle or from a special trailer, if a two-car unit were required. They were employed in a variety of different ways, including local services along main lines in both urban and rural areas, as well as on branch lines where traffic was light. The distances over which they worked were generally short, and a through service from Chippenham to Salisbury and back, about forty miles each way, was probably very much an exception.

The first two steam rail-motors were put into service along the Stroud Valley between Stonehouse and Chalford on 12th October 1903. In addition to calling at the two intermediate stations at Stroud and Brimscombe, they also stopped at four halts established where roads or footpaths crossed the line. The halts were rudimentary, the 'platform' consisting of a space at the side of the line which had been cleared of vegetation, marked out with old sleepers, and the area filled in with ballast or gravel. No shelter was provided at the lineside, and tickets were issued by the guard. The cars were fitted with retractable steps to enable passengers to board and alight at the halts. The service provided in the Stroud Valley was a great success. It was later extended to Gloucester, and two

A railmotor arriving at Perivale Halt on duty 'C' which entailed 181 miles daily.   *British Railways*

more halts were added in 1904 and 1905, and yet another halt in 1930.

At the beginning of May 1904 rail-motors were introduced in the London area with services between Westbourne Park and Southall, running via North Acton, Greenford and Hanwell. At the same time they inaugurated a half-hourly service between Southall and Brentford, a regular-interval service of this frequency being still some-

thing of a novelty on the railways at this time, particularly on the GWR. They also operated services from Southall over the North London Railway as far as Willesden Junction, and over the West London line between Southall and Victoria. In June 1904 a frequent service was instituted in the Plymouth area between Plympton, Millbay and Saltash, three halts being provided initially, and a fourth in 1905.

Northolt Halt showing the 'pagoda' type shelters on the platforms.   *Lens of Sutton*

Railmotor at Stanley Bridge Halte between Chippenham and Calne.

Lens of Sutton

Built for the benefit of the Royal Navy, Defiance Halt,
near Plymouth, was constructed by sailors.

GWR Magazine

On 2nd January 1905 a service was introduced between Kidderminster, Bewdley, Stourport and Hartlebury, and with its frequent reversals, it clearly demonstrated the value of being able to drive a train from either end. Thereafter, expansion was rapid, and during 1905 rail-motors became established on several lines in the Birmingham area, including the branch to Stourbridge Town, from Oldbury to Langley Green, and from Old Hill to both Dudley and Halesowen. Elsewhere they pioneered a network of new services radiating from Wrexham, and were introduced locally in Wiltshire and the West Country. Ultimately there were few parts of the system where they did not put in an appearance.

Before 1905 was out, however, auto-train working was introduced. This involved the working of trailers from the

rail-motors by small tank locomotives on a push-and-pull basis. The locomotives chosen to be fitted for the purpose were mainly 0—4—2T, although for some parts of the system the 0—6—0T was preferred. In this way, up to two trailers could be worked at either end of the locomotive, whereas a rail-motor could handle only one trailer, and that often with some difficulty. The success of the new service in developing traffic in the Plymouth area did much to hasten the introduction of the auto-train, which became a familiar feature of the GWR scene for many years.

Although rail-motors were not to disappear from the GWR until 1935, their use entailed a number of limiting factors. For example, repairs to the engine of a rail-motor might necessitate the temporary withdrawal of the complete vehicle, and it might become difficult to maintain the service with an ordinary engine and a trailer, more so if an ordinary coach had to be used as well. On branch lines, too, it was often useful to have a separate locomotive, which could also undertake any shunting required, and which could work the goods traffic, either independently or as a mixed train with a passenger trailer next to the engine.

Nevertheless, if it were working on its own, a rail-motor might be required to take an additional vehicle in exceptional circumstances. On the first day of services through to Winchcombe from Honeybourne, a rail-motor arrived at Winchcombe drawing a saloon carriage from Paddington with passengers *en route* to Sudeley Castle nearby.

Such was the success of the rail-motors that in the first half of 1905 it was reported that they had carried

2,250,000 passengers, a figure which increased to
3,500,000 in the second half of the same year. Such
traffic required some improvement in the rudimentary
facilities at halts, with which the services had been commenced in the Stroud Valley. Some of the later halts
were provided with a platform about ten inches above
rail level, so that steps were still needed for passengers,
but others had a platform at the standard height of 3 ft 0 in
above rail level. All the halts at ground level had received
a platform of one or other of these dimensions by 1915,
and most had received platforms of standard height by
1923. Waiting shelters also became general. Some were of
timber, but on platforms of standard height, they were
often made of corrugated iron to a design which caused
them to be nick-named 'pagodas'.

It was at the half-yearly general meeting in August
1903 that the chairman announced the intention of the
company to move into the field of motor bus services,
which he regarded as logical feeders to the railway. Their
introduction was indeed then imminent and the first of the
services, that between Helston and the Lizard, began on
the 17th of the same month. The venture proved highly
successful, and by the middle of 1910 nearly 80 vehicles
were working on more than 300 route miles, extending
into about 15 counties. They were controlled from a

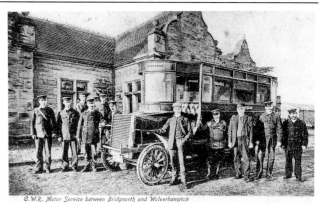

G.W.R. Motor Service between Bridgnorth and Wolverhampton

GWR motor bus for Wolverhampton at Bridgnorth station.

Lens of Sutton

headquarters at Slough. In some instances, the mails were
also carried.

The services included one between Lampeter and
Aberayron, but this was replaced by a light railway which
was opened in 1911. Replacement by a railway was
doubtless also expected for the service between Wolverhampton and Bridgnorth but this was not to be. This
latter service was operated in later years by Wolverhampton

GWR sightseeing motor bus outside Buckingham Palace, 1908.

BBC Hulton Picture Library

Metropolitan Railway electric locomotives outside Paddington, used for working suburban trains from Paddington through to the City, 1910.   *BBC Hulton Picture Library*

Corporation, but its railway antecedents remained clear to the discerning eye as it continued to terminate in Wolverhampton at the GWR (Low Level) station.

Quickly realising the potential of motor vehicles for tourist sightseeing in London, the company inaugurated such a facility on 22nd August 1907. The tour was operated in conjunction with the Motor Jobmasters' Association, running twice daily from Paddington station on two days a week, accompanied by a 'guide-lecturer'. The Motor Jobmasters doubtless supplied a suitable vehicle for the tours which continued for the remainder of the summer season. Similar tours were operated for the summer season of 1908, when the company had a suitable vehicle of its own, and again in 1909 increased to three days a week.

Also realised was the potential of motor vehicles as emergency replacement for trains. In 1907, when a fall of rock in Malvern tunnel caused the temporary closure of the railway, GWR buses from Slough were used to provide a replacement service between Great Malvern and Colwall, and the climb over the Malvern Hills must have provided a gruelling test for these early vehicles. Towards the end of 1909 buses were used for three days, replacing the trains on the Brixham branch while the track was relaid.

The GWR also set out to encourage the private motorist to avail himself of the short cut offered by the Severn Tunnel, as compared with the long detour through Gloucester. Arrangements were introduced in April 1909 whereby special wagons for the conveyance of cars would be kept at Pilning and Severn Tunnel Junction, and by the end of the year it was reported that more than 300 cars had been handled at Pilning. There was some concern over the fire risk from allowing petrol to remain in the tanks of cars during conveyance, so provision was made for petrol to be emptied into a store before conveyance, and for it

to be replaced with a similar quantity on the arrival of the car at the other side.

The first decade of the century saw the GWR involved with electrification, albeit to a very modest extent. The line concerned was the Hammersmith & City which had been vested in the GW and Metropolitan Railway Companies jointly in 1867. The extent of the joint ownership was from a point close to the east end of Westbourne Park station to Hammersmith, together with a branch from Latimer Road to join the West London Railway at Uxbridge Road. At the beginning of the century there was a basic service of eight passenger trains an hour each way through Westbourne Park, six running between Hammersmith and Aldgate or New Cross, and two between Addison Road and Aldgate. To obtain access from the joint line at Westbourne Park to the purely Metropolitan line east of Bishop's Road, Paddington, the trains used nearly a mile of line which was GWR property. Royal Oak station was on this section.

In view of the intensity of the service over its lines, the Metropolitan was keen to adopt electric traction and had done so on its Inner Circle Line in 1905. It was hardly likely, therefore, to accept willingly a continuation of the steam trains to and from Hammersmith. Accordingly, the two companies agreed a scheme for electrification and improvement. This included the erection by the GWR of an electricity generating station at Park Royal which would not only supply current for the newly electrified line, but also provide light and power for a large part of the GWR installations around Paddington. The GWR also undertook responsibility for building new carriage sheds at Hammersmith, using the distinctive red brick which is such a feature of the company's building works of the period. These sheds remain in use for London Transport trains. Some of the stations on the line, notably Hammer-

The approaches to Paddington near Ranelagh Bridge, showing the electrified lines for use by trains on the Hammersmith & City service.

Exterior of District Railway station at Ealing Broadway, 1912. *British Railways*

An earlier Metropolitan Railway locomotive at Paddington, 1910. *BBC Hulton Picture Library*

The growth in goods traffic over the decade required the construction of new marshalling yards such as this one at Stoke Gifford, near Bristol.

Collection John Lewis

smith itself and Ladbroke Grove, also have many GWR features of the period.

The conductor rails were energized on the morning of 1st October 1906 and in the early hours of the following morning a trial trip was made with a multiple-unit electric train from Bishop's Road to Hammersmith. On 5th November the first electric trains went into public use, gradually replacing steam trains over the following few weeks. The steam trains had been provided by the two companies individually but the new electric stock was owned jointly, being lettered *Hammersmith & City Railway* with the names of the owning companies. To emphasise the equality of the interest, the names of the two companies were placed in one order on one side of the coaches, and in the reverse order on the other.

While the electrification works had been proceeding, the GWR had promoted a bill for its Ealing & Shepherds Bush Railway, which received the royal assent in 1905. This was to make connection with the original main line at Ealing Broadway and with the new line to High Wycombe at North Acton, pass under the original main line, and terminate at two junctions, one with the Central London Railway at Wood Lane and the other with the West London Railway at Viaduct Junction. The company was at pains to emphasise that the purpose of the new line was to enable traffic to be worked to the West London Railway without the need for the conflicting movements required at West London Junction. At the half-yearly meeting in February 1905 the chairman stated that it

would not be worked by electricity, but that the trains using it would run over other parts of the system and would be worked by steam.

In the ultimate conductor rails were laid for Central London trains, although it was 1920 before they commenced in service between Wood Lane and Ealing Broadway. GW goods traffic by way of Viaduct Junction had commenced in 1917 but the line was not used extensively by the GWR, although in the early 1920s it had a workmen's train from Addison Road to Ealing Broadway and Greenford, and back.

And so the question has to be asked, what were the results of all the effort and expenditure which had spanned a decade and more. The growth in traffic in the years prior to 1900 has been noted already, so what happened after 1900? The following figures for goods traffic speak largely for themselves:-

Year	Carried – tons millions			From 1900 Change %	Train miles millions	From 1900 Change %
	Minerals	Merchandise	Total			
1900	30.1	7.4	37.5	—	23.1	—
1902	32.8	7.8	40.6	+ 8.2	22.1	− 4.3
1904	35.2	7.5	42.7	+ 13.8	20.2	− 12.7
1906	37.7	7.9	45.6	+ 21.5	19.6	− 15.4
1908	42.4	8.2	50.6	+ 35.1	19.9	− 13.9
1910	44.7	8.7	53.4	+ 42.5	19.8	− 14.5
1912	44.3	10.0	54.3	+ 44.8	19.6	− 15.1

It will be seen that in 1912 the tonnage of goods carried showed an increase of nearly one half over the figure for 1900, while over the same period the train

This view shows part of the goods yard at Reading lying on the north side of the line near the station. Reading Central was built to relieve pressure here. Wagons owned by local coal merchants are much in evidence, as also wagons for coal from the Wyken Colliery near Coventry.

British Railways

Passengers waiting for an up workmen's train at Southall, then identified also as Brentford Junction. The passenger service between Southall and Brentford was withdrawn in 1942; in the Edwardian period a half-hourly service of railmotors had been provided.

British Railways

mileage fell by 15%. The goods train mileage of 1900 was the highest reported by the company, certainly up to the exceptional war-time conditions of 1914 to 1918. It may be argued that mileage fell, possibly because more coal was being worked over short distances to the South Wales ports. Indeed, the inclusion of the figures for the Rhondda & Swansea Bay and Port Talbot Railways for the first time during 1907 and 1908, all short-haul traffic, may have had some effect on comparisons. In spite of these factors, however, it is impossible to escape the conclusion that mileage fell very largely because more powerful locomotives were hauling heavier trains over the new and skilfully-engineered main lines. Without such improvements, parts of the system could well have become completely choked with traffic, and the economic growth of the nation would have suffered.

In monetary terms, there was also a marked improvement in efficiency. Receipts per goods train-mile rose from approx. £0.25 in 1900 to approx. £0.38 in 1912, and this was achieved when the receipts from coal and coke traffic showed very little increase in total, in spite of the growth in tonnage. The average receipt per ton of coal and coke was, in fact, generally falling throughout the period, possibly some indication of a reduction in the average distance over which it was carried.

Passenger traffic figures are given in the table alongside.

The number of passengers carried in 1908 represented the peak for the company in its pre-1914 history. From 1900 to 1908 the growth in the number of passengers carried had been in line with that achieved in the previous

ten years. In those previous ten years, however, the rate of growth in the number of passengers had exceeded the rate of growth in the mileage of passenger trains, but after 1900 the reverse was the case. Published statistics show that 49,000 season tickets were in use in 1900, rising to 214,000 in 1912, but their equivalent in numbers of passengers is not stated, neither is the full impact of the traffic generated by rail-motors and auto-trains. The fall in 1912 was attributed largely to a coal strike in that year but by then it must be assumed that the street tramcar was attracting local traffic away from the railway in some of the larger towns. What is certain, however, is that passengers over the period travelled in greater comfort, at greater speed, and with increased choice of services. And from the modest increase in the receipts per passenger over the period, the average distance travelled was gradually increasing.

Year	Passengers carried * millions	From 1900 change %	Train miles millions	From 1900 change %
1900	80.9	—	23.3	—
1902	80.9	—	24.5	+ 5.1
1904	87.1	+ 7.5	26.7	+ 14.9
1906	93.3	+ 15.2	28.2	+ 21.3
1908	104.9	+ 29.6	30.3	+ 30.1
1910	104.0	+ 28.5	30.6	+ 31.4
1912	98.6	+ 21.8	28.6	+ 23.0

* Excluding holders of season tickets

A busy scene at Paddington in 1908.

British Railways

Off for the Holidays

August 1910

An immaculately groomed 'Star' class No. 4021 *King Edward* before working the funeral train of the late King to Windsor in May 1910.   *BBC Hulton Picture Library*

Although King Edward VII died on 6th May 1910, the 'Edwardian' age might be said to have lasted a little longer. Throughout the country, and indeed the Empire, things continued in much the same way, although there was increasing disruption within the British Isles with workers demanding better wages and conditions. In the summer of 1911 there was a national railway strike, albeit of only two days' duration, whilst problems in Ireland over the proposed Home Rule Bill and the women's suffrage movement tended to cloud the illusion of a 'golden age'. On the Great Western, too, the passing, in 1911, of Sir James Inglis signified the end of an era of dramatic change with uncompleted and abandoned schemes. It is impossible to speculate which direction the company would have taken following this loss, for a single pistol shot, at Sarajevo in far-away Austria-Hungary, in 1914 changed the course of history, not only for the GWR, but for the whole world.